Guides: 26

SEASHORE LIFE

OF

SOUTHERN CALIFORNIA

An Introduction to the Animal Life
of California Beaches South of Santa Barbara

BY

SAM HINTON

Illustrated by the author

UNIVERSITY OF CALIFORNIA PRESS

BERKELEY, LOS ANGELES, LONDON

CALIFORNIA NATURAL HISTORY GUIDES

Arthur C. Smith, General Editor

UNIVERSITY OF CALIFORNIA PRESS
BERKELEY AND LOS ANGELES, CALIFORNIA
UNIVERSITY OF CALIFORNIA PRESS, LTD.
LONDON, ENGLAND

CONTENTS

[3]

INTRODUCTION

The sea is wet and the land is dry, but the line separating them is never the same from one moment to the next. With every spent wave the boundaries are altered; with every rise and fall of the tide, the ocean surrenders or conquers some of its realm. And the very sands of the beach move in and out with the seasons so that in some summers a man may walk the beach with his feet higher than his head would have been a few months earlier.

The dividing line between the sea and the land, then, is not really a line at all; it is an area, a zone, a dominion in its own right. Partaking in some measure of both earth and water, it belongs wholly to neither. Because its upper and lower limits are defined by the extremes of the tides, we speak of it as the "intertidal zone." This book is an introduction to some of the features of this zone and its contiguous waters, and to a selected few of the thousands of creatures that may be seen there.

One task of science is to peel away layer after layer of mystery from the natural world, as if to get ever closer to an imaginary core of "truth." But diminishing the mystery need not diminish the sense of wonder and delight; enjoyment and knowledge can — and should — increase together. Anyone can love the sea, and feel restored in the presence of its sights and sounds and smells, without recourse to a book. But a book may add an intellectual spice to a basic emotion, and that is what I hope this book will do.

The aim is to provide a sort of beach-walker's guide, giving a general picture, with a few added details, of the Southern California shore and its abundant life. It will be successful if some of its readers are led to seek information beyond what can be provided here. A selected list of references will be found at the end of this book.

THE TIDES

The slow rise and fall of the sea, in a complex but predictable pattern, has long appealed to man's imagination. The tidal rhythm was once explained as the result of the regular breathing of some tremendous sea monster, or as the breathing of the living sea itself. The true explanation is perhaps even more romantic: the tides are brought about by the far-off sun and moon.

Every object in the universe exerts a gravitational pull upon every other object, the magnitude depending upon the masses of the objects and the distance between them. Our solar system is an assemblage of such mutually attracted bodies, held together by the force of gravity, but prevented from falling into each other by the centrifugal forces of their respective orbits about the sun. The earth is thus held near the sun because of mutual gravitational pull, and kept away from the sun by centrifugal force. In the same way the position of the earth and the moon represents a balance of these two forces.

Throughout the system as a whole, these forces are in exact balance, but local variations allow one or the other of them to be more strongly felt in a given time and place. Gravitational attraction is directed to the center of mass of each of the heavenly bodies involved. The surface of the sea is some 4,000 miles away from this center, so that the attraction of the sun and moon are not the same on the sea as they are on the earth as a whole.

We must remember that it is incorrect to think of the earth as stationary while the moon orbits around it; they actually revolve around a common center. If the two bodies were of equal mass, this center would lie halfway between them. As it is, the earth is many times the more massive, and the common center lies 1,000 miles beneath the earth's surface, or 3,000 miles from its actual center. So the motion of the earth-moon system is around this center of orbital motion. (It should be pointed out that this has nothing to do with the day-night motion of the earth on its own axis.) The results of this motion were summed up, with apologies to Christina, by a well-known physicist who is also Dean of the College of Letters and Science at the Berkeley campus of the University of California:

"Who has weighed the moon?
    Neither you nor I;
But the solid earth is wobbling
    As the moon goes tumbling by."

This wobble of the earth's is of the greatest importance in the variations of the tide-producing forces. At a point centered directly under the moon, the moon's gravitational attraction is felt more strongly

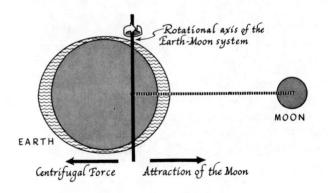

Rotational axis of the Earth-Moon system

MOON

EARTH

Centrifugal Force   Attraction of the Moon

than is the centrifugal force; at the point on the opposite side of the earth, the reverse is true, and here the centrifugal force is the stronger. In both places, the basic result is the same: there is an element of the balanced system which is directed outward, away from the earth's center. This outward force is only one nine-millionth as great as that of the earth's gravity, but is nevertheless enough to cause the waters to bulge out at these two points, creating a zone of high tide on both sides of the globe.

Between the two high tide points there is a band where low tides prevail. Since the earth revolves on its own axis once a day, a given spot will pass once through two high tide points and two low tide zones with every complete rotation. The moon is moving in its orbit in this same direction, so that by the time the spot on earth makes one revolution, the moon has progressed a little, and more time is needed to catch up with it. Thus the period from one high tide to the next (or from low to low) is about 12 hours and 25 minutes. In each period of about 24 hours and 50

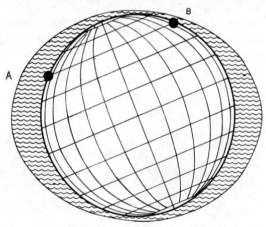

minutes, there are two high tides and two low tides.

The earth's axis is tilted in relation to the plane of its orbit, so that specific locations pass through different portions of the tide zones. Thus the two high tides on one day are of quite different heights, and the same is true of the two lows.

Many other factors combine to cause variations in the height of the tides. The moon, for example, varies in its distance from the earth, thus changing its gravitational effects upon the sea. Also, the moon wanders toward the north and south, changing its position relative to the earth's equator. Still more important is that the sun raises a tidal bulge of its own which is not always in the same place as that caused by the moon. When the bulges coincide, the differences between high and low tide are greatest; when a moon high tide coincides with a sun low tide, the two partially cancel one another, and low tide and high tide are not very far apart. Near the time of the full moon and the new moon, the earth, moon, and sun are lined up, and the tide-producing forces work together. At such

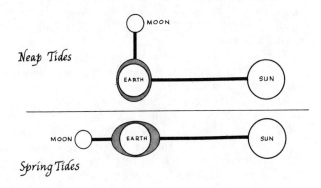

times, there is a great difference between high tide and low tide, and these are known as "spring" tides—not in relation to a season, but from an old Anglo-Saxon word meaning, among other things, "to leap."

During the moon's quarters, the three heavenly bodies are not lined up, but form a right angle, and the separate effects of the sun and moon fight one another. The high tides then are not very high, and the lows are not very low, and these are known as "neap" tides. This word too is from the Anglo-Saxon, and signifies something "scarce."

Tides are affected by the phenomenon of resonance. Each mass of water has its own natural period of oscillation, and even in the open sea the water has a tendency to divide itself into various complex bodies, each one oscillating at its own rate. This propensity is emphasized in partially enclosed bodies of water. If the natural oscillatory period of a body of water coincides with the repeated gravitational pull of the sun or moon, the oscillation will be magnified. The water in the Bay of Fundy, for example, is of such a size and shape as to be "in resonance" with some of the astronomical forces, with the result that the tide there may rise and fall more than 60 feet. Similarly, at the head of the Gulf of California, the tide range is at least 24 feet.

The astronomical factor of gravitational attraction plus the local factors of resonance and reflection give us our complex tide situation. Along the California coast, there are two high tides and two low tides every day, although occasionally there will be only three tides in one calendar day, with the next one coming right after midnight; this is because the tidal day (the lunar day) is more than 24 hours. One of these highs is quite a bit higher than the other, and one of the lows is lower. These extremes in the tide are called "higher high water," "lower high water," "higher low water," and "lower low water." To provide a frame of reference for mariners who must maneuver their vessels into and out of shallow harbors, an arbitrary sea level, known as "zero tide," has been selected, and the tide height is reported as above or below this zero line. On this coast, it developed that the most useful place for zero was at mean lower low water; that is, all of the lower low tides for a long period of time are averaged, and their mean level is designated as the zero point. On the Atlantic coast, both of the daily lows are at about the same level, and zero there is the mean of *all* the low waters.

The collector or observer of seashore life waits for those tides that are expressed as being "below zero." These are the "minus" tides, and they expose parts of the shore usually covered with water. In Southern California, the tide situation is such that these minus tides in midwinter usually occur in the middle of the afternoon, while in summer they come in the wee small hours before dawn. This makes a great deal of difference in the planning of field trips!

Daily and weekly tide predictions are given in most newspapers in seacoast towns; tide books for the entire year may be obtained at marine hardware stores or at service stations catering to boats. These predictions are taken from the tide tables published annually by the U. S. Department of Commerce, Coast and Geodetic Survey.

The selection of a living-place by most intertidal animals is based at least partly upon the relative length of time of exposure to the air. Those creatures making their homes high up on the rocks, for example, are covered with water only a few times during the year; conversely, those attached to rocks or pier pilings a foot or so below the zero level are exposed to the air very infrequently, and for short periods of time even then. Between these two extremes lies a whole gamut of exposure, and it is often possible to estimate the state of the tide by identifying the animals occur-

[11]

ring at what is now the water's edge. This matter of tide-zone distribution will be discussed in a later section.

WAVES

Ocean waves are born in storms, and travel from the storm areas to the far shores of the sea. Waves breaking on Southern California shores may have traveled halfway around the globe, or they may come from nearby storms.

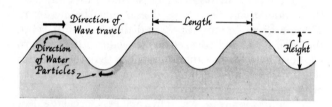

In the open sea, waves differ from one another in height (the vertical distance from trough to crest) and in length (the distance from one crest to the succeeding one). They differ also in the speed at which they travel (period), but this is entirely a function of their length, and does not vary independently; the longer the wave, the faster it travels.

Where the waves originate in a storm area, the sea surface is confused, and no regular wave pattern is visible. In all this confusion, waves of many lengths are being produced, and these travel away from the storm, with each wavelength moving at its own fixed speed. By the time they have gone some distance, they have begun sorting themselves; the faster-moving long waves will have outdistanced the shorter, slower ones. Waves thus arrive at a distant shore in the form of a quite regular swell, presenting an appearance very unlike that of the patternless "sea" within the

[12]

storm area. If all the sea were calm except for one single storm somewhere, the distant pattern would be even more regular than it is; in actual fact, however, we are always seeing waves from a number of sources, so that the swell has a certain irregularity. Each train of waves is superimposed upon other trains. When two or more crests coincide, the swell at that moment is high; conversely, when a major crest coincides with a major trough, the swell at that time is low.

If you watch the surfers in the water, you will see how they wait while a number of low swells pass them, and finally "catch" one of the big ones of the series. Fishermen too make use of this, only they wait for the low part of a series before putting their skiffs out through the surf. Various tales are told of the magic numbers by means of which one may predict the high or low waves; some insist that every seventh wave is a bigger one, while others say it is every ninth.

There is, of course, no wave-cycle that consistently coincides with such numbers, but like many traditional beliefs, this one is founded on a core of truth—the truth being that waves reach shore in high groups and low groups. From a statistical viewpoint, over a long period of time the chances are that one wave in every 25 will be twice as high as the average wave-height during that period, while one in every 1,175 will be three times the average.

Observation of some of the variable characteristics of waves can provide knowledge of other less easily observed ones. For the person standing on the shore, the easiest variable to measure is the period—the time between two successive crests. Other factors, such as length and velocity, change as a wave moves into shallow water and breaks, but the period remains the same. And this period can tell you the velocity and the length as they were while the wave was still

[13]

in deep water. Remember that the speed of a wave in deep water is determined only by its length; that is, a wave of a certain length can travel only at a certain speed, and so will take a certain time to pass a point. A wave whose length is about 245 feet will travel, in deep water, at a speed of about 21 knots (or a little over 24 miles per hour), and the time between successive crests will always be about 7 seconds. This relationship is constant. The velocity in knots is always three times the period in seconds ($v=3t$), and the wavelength in feet is five times the period squared ($l=5t^2$).

Still more information may be gained if you can estimate the height of a wave, although an accurate measurement here is quite a bit harder to come by. The easiest way is to observe the waves against a pier piling beyond the breakers, and estimate the distance between the highest and lowest points marked by a passing wave. Using wave length and height as identifying features, physical oceanographers have back-tracked wave trains, and have found that their source may often be indicated by certain combinations of height, period, and season.

SEASON	HEIGHT	PERIOD	SOURCE
Spring	9 to 14 ft.	5 to 7 sec.	Local storms
Summer	3 to 6 ft.	6 to 9 sec.	Winds surrounding a high-pressure area to the west.
Summer	6 to 9 ft.	13 to 20 sec.	Storms in the Roaring 40's, 40° south of the Equator.
Winter	5 to 12 ft.	7 to 10 sec.	Storm fronts approaching from the west.

The water itself does not move along with a wave. Water particles move in vertical circles, going forward at the crest of the wave and backward in the trough. For water particles at the surface, the diameter of the described circle is equal to the height of the waves; deeper particles move in smaller circles until, at a depth of about seven times the wavelength, there is virtually no water motion at all. If the water is much less than seven wavelengths deep, the circular motion of the particles is interfered with, and the wave begins to behave in a different manner: it slows down, its crests become closer together, and it becomes steeper and taller until its top finally topples forward. It has then become what we call a "breaker," and the breakers are collectively known as "surf." Breakers usually begin to form where the water is about 1⅓ times as deep as the wave is high, although where there is a bottom with a strong break to its slope, or where there is a strong wind blowing toward shore, the waves may break in water twice as deep as the breaker height.

Unlike the water in an open-ocean wave, the water in a breaker is actually moving with the wave, and as a result, water is literally piled up on the beach. During a heavy surf, sea level right next to the shore may be as much as three feet higher than wave level out beyond the breakers. This water cannot remain here, of course, and must flow out to sea again. This it does as a rip current. Rip currents are narrow streams of water flowing rapidly seaward, and they constitute a serious hazard to inexperienced bathers. At times, the flow is sufficiently strong to scour out a channel in the beach sand, so that someone wading in shallow water may suddenly step off over his depth, and be swept out to sea.

If you should ever be caught in a rip current, it is quite easy to escape if you know how to swim and don't panic. Just swim at right angles to the current— parallel to the shore—and you will soon be out of it, and free to turn toward the beach again.

Rip currents are often called "riptides," but as they are in no way connected with the true cyclic tides, this term is needlessly confusing. Another confusing word is "undertow," which is supposed to connote a strong current running seaward along the bottom; the under-

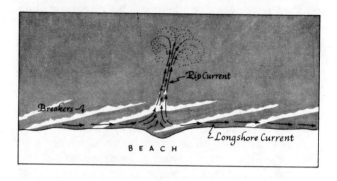

tow is said to pull swimmers under as it carries them away from shore. Actually, less than 1 percent of the piled-up beach water flows back along the bottom, and undertow is mainly imaginary.

The fact that entering shallow water causes a wave to slow down gives rise to all sorts of phenomena connected with refraction. For instance, when a wave approaches the shore at an angle, the portion of the wave first "feeling the bottom" is slowed down, and this swings the wave around until its crest is more nearly parallel to the shore at that point.

Where a submarine ridge extends out from shore, the part of a wave that is over the ridge travels more slowly than the parts on either side, and this causes a focusing of wave-energy toward the landward end of the submerged ridge. Sailing men have known of this for thousands of years, and have steered clear of headlands, as headlands usually mark the location of submarine ridges.

Conversely, a submarine canyon *spreads* the wave-energy, so that the surf at a canyon head is lower than it is elsewhere in that vicinity. Knowledge of this, too, is part of the lore of seafaring men, and small fishing boats are traditionally launched in such areas.

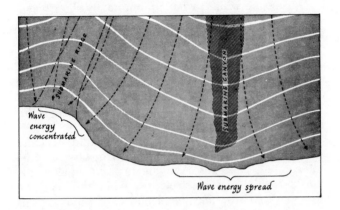

The refractive power of the beach slope is not always enough to turn waves completely parallel to the shore, and some waves do arrive at an angle. This is an important factor in the formation and maintenance of sandy beaches.

Waves of a short period are the most effective ones in moving beach sand, and most such waves in Southern California come in from the northwest. Being short, they are not as much affected by the changes in the bottom contours as other waves are, and they strike the beach at a considerable angle. This sets up local currents moving south along the shore; there are limited areas with a northward flow occurring intermittently, but the net movement is southerly. The sand stirred up by these waves is therefore carried toward the south.

In addition to the currents, another factor of the oblique waves creates a southward movement of sand particles. Breakers from these waves rush at an angle up the beach, carrying sand with them; their energy spent, they drain back to the sea in a straight downhill line. Thus a grain of surface sand may move several feet to the south with each breaking wave.

During the winter, when appropriately short waves are coming in from the frequent northerly storms, a lot of sand is removed from the beach to form a low bar, well offshore. Then, when summer comes, its longer waves carry the sand to shore again and deposit it at a point considerably south of where it had been before. In some places, the seasonal rise and fall of the beach sand may be over six feet, although this doesn't happen every year.

Where a man-made riprap or other solid structure extends out from the beach, the flow of sand may be interrupted. This causes the sand to build out along the northern sides of such structures, while the beach on the southern side may be denuded of sand. This is because new sand coming down from the north is stopped by the structure and remains on the upstream side; downstream, sand is carried away and not replaced.

Breakwaters in the form of small islands parallel to the shore reduce the force of the waves striking that shore, so that less sand is scoured out. The beach line then has a tendency to bend outward toward the breakwater, and several such structures—intended to provide a safe anchorage for small boats—have ended up as peninsula-tips rather than islands.

CURRENTS

In addition to the small local alongshore currents already discussed, there are ocean currents of far greater magnitude; these are extremely important as controllers of climate and distributors of marine organisms. Off our coast, the most important current of this sort is the California Current, a cold mass of water some 400 miles wide, moving southward at 0.2 to 0.6 miles per hour. As ocean currents go, this is not a tremendous one, moving only about 1/10 as much water as the great Gulf Stream of the Atlantic. Nevertheless, it moves a lot of water—more than 200 times as much as the Mississippi River, or about 3 times as much as all the earth's rivers combined!

It is sometimes believed that our main current should be called the Japanese Current, but this is incorrect. The Japanese Current, or Kuroshio, is a *warm* current flowing northward on the western side of the Pacific, while the California Current is *cold* and flows south on the eastern side. Its temperature averages 2 degrees C. cooler than the surrounding water, and this difference has a profound tempering effect upon the Pacific Coast climate.

A zone of complex and variable water movements is found between the shore and the near edge of the California Current. During the winter, for instance, this area often has a north-flowing current with a speed of as much as 1½ miles per hour. And at times there is instead a vast eddy, often more than 100 miles in diameter, rotating counterclockwise at a rate of one revolution in 20 to 40 days. Factors such as these have a direct bearing upon the distribution of such creatures as sardines, whose floating eggs are completely at the mercy of the currents.

In any movement of a large mass, such as the water in a current, the rotation of the earth imparts what appears to be a deflective force to the right. (In the southern hemisphere, it is to the left.) This means that in our main southbound current, there is an element of movement tending toward the west, away from the shore. The water in this current is mainly near the surface, and as it veers away from shore it is replaced by water welling up from below; close to shore, therefore, there is frequently an "upwelling" of cold bottom water. This is particularly obvious to the swimmer during some of the "Santa Ana" periods, when a hot, dry wind blows from the east and hastens the surface flow away from the shore.

This upwelling has a number of effects. For one thing, the deep cold water is rich in trace elements demanded by plants, and the sea off Southern California is characterized by a profusion of marine plants —both the stationary seaweeds and the microscopic planktonic plants. This floral abundance leads to an abundance of animal life, since plants are the basic energy-source for all animals, and it should be noted that the major fisheries of the temperate zones are located where upwelling is a common feature.

The cold water near shore has another effect, this one upon our climate and weather. It often happens, especially in winter, that a mass of warm dry air moves out from the land and goes several miles out to sea, where it just sits for a while. The lower part of such an air column is cooled by contact with the water; at the same time, it soaks up moisture. Both of these activities increase the density of the lower air and help form a stable inversion. This allows the process to continue until finally the air next to the water is almost as cool as the water, and has soaked up all the moisture it can contain at that temperature. Finally, when the sea breeze brings this air toward the land, it meets the zone of colder water near the shore, and its temperature is still further lowered. Colder air cannot contain as much moisture as warmer air, so now there is *more* water than can remain in our air mass, and the excess is precipitated in the form of fog. This is the occasion of the spectacular sharp walls of fog that move on to the coast on so many winter afternoons. Viewed objectively, these advancing fogs are among the more spectacular of natural wonders, and can only be described as beautiful; try to remember that as you shiver in your car, creeping home from the beach.

[20]

THE CHEMISTRY OF SEA WATER

Water, which seems to us the blandest and gentlest of liquids, is really the most corrosive substance known. It dissolves more kinds of materials, and in greater quantity, than any other liquid. Since practically all the water on earth eventually finds its way to the sea, carrying dissolved material with it, it is not surprising that sea water is an extremely complex mixture that has been well characterized as "a dilute solution of practically everything."

The chief mineral constituents of sea water are certain salts, and while the total amount of such salts may vary to some extent, their proportions, as measured against one another, remain remarkably constant. In each thousand parts of sea water, the total salts may constitute 34 to 36 parts, but there is not this much variation in the proportions. Thus, for each 19 parts of chlorine there will always be 11 parts of sodium, 1 part of magnesium, 0.9 parts of sulfur, 0.3 of calcium, a little less than that of potassium, and so on. These ratios are so constant that the chemical oceanographer need only measure the amount of chlorine in order to know the exact amounts of the other major constituents.

This equilibrium of salts is surprising in the light of the facts that new salts are continually being brought to the sea in rivers, that the proportions of salts in river water are very different from those in the sea, and that the salts remain in the sea when the water evaporates and is recycled. As an example of the difference in the chemical composition of river water as opposed to sea water, we would find that, if we extracted a pound of salts from river water, about 60 percent of it consisted of carbonates, especially in the form of calcium carbonate. In the same amount of sea-salt, however, carbonates would constitute only about 0.3 percent of the weight. These differences, together with the steady state of sea water, are probably accounted for by the abundant life processes going on in the sea. There has probably been a further conditioning by long-past events, as when the seas' edges have intruded over vast stretches of flat coastal lands so as to form broad shallows in which complex differential precipitation occurred as evaporation was intensified.

Dissolved gases in the sea are subject to considerable variation, with a consequent effect upon animal and plant life. Oxygen content, for example, may vary from zero, as at the bottoms of certain fjords, to the more usual 8.5 parts per thousand. Carbon dioxide, necessary to plants, also has a wide range, but is always many times more abundant than in air. There is a constant exchange of carbon dioxide between the sea and the air, with atmospheric quantities stabilized by the great reservoir of the sea. This stability is of the greatest importance to the climate of the whole world, as small changes in atmospheric carbon dioxide can result in large changes in ground temperature.

Many other types of chemicals are important in sea water, even though they are found there in minute quantities. Some living things have the ability to extract certain of these elements with an efficiency that is quite astonishing; they can build up in their bodies concentrations of rare materials to a proportion hundreds of times greater than that in the surrounding waters. Some tunicates (sea-squirts) do this with vanadium; molluscs concentrate copper; radiolarians, strontium; jellyfishes, tin, lead, and zinc; while certain sponges and seaweeds take up iodine. Sometimes it is relatively easy for humans to remove these substances from the tissues of these living things, as when we extract iodine from kelp, when it would be neither feasible nor profitable to take them directly from the water.

Complex molecules based on various combinations

of carbon with other elements constitute what are known as "organic" compounds, and they are the stuff of which living tissue is made. Such molecules, in the form of dissolved organic matter, are fairly abundant in sea water, and are necessary to the growth of marine plants. Phosphates and nitrates—the "fertilizers"—occur in varying quantities, and their abundance determines the distribution of the plants; without them, no plants can grow. Abundant sea life is found only where there is an adequate supply of these materials, and where there is a cycling that returns them to the water for further use. Indeed, the whole process of life in the sea — or anywhere else — may be viewed as a cycling and recycling of these trace elements, used in such a way as to distribute a finite quantity of energy among the living things that use it.

THE CYCLE OF LIFE IN THE SEA

The complete dependence of all animals upon plants, and the dependence of plants upon sunlight and certain chemicals, point up the fact that all life is interrelated, and that the relationships are particularly obvious in the ocean.

Living is a process that uses energy, and this energy has its origin in the sun. Animals, however, have no way of using the sun's energy directly, and, through eating plants, must obtain it second hand. Plants make use of solar energy to power the process of photosynthesis, by means of which carbon dioxide and water and trace elements are combined into complex organic chemicals in which a surplus of energy is stored. Animals eating these plants, or eating other animals that have eaten the plants, release some of this stored energy for their own use.

Every marine community has its own complex chain of life, which is a means of distributing solar energy. In a mussel bed, for example, energy is supplied to the animals in the form of floating planktonic life, as

[23]

well as suspended particles of detrital organic matter. The mussels themselves feed by passing water through their gills and straining out edible material. The many little creatures that find shelter among the firmly attached mussels feed on plankton, detritus, or the encrusting mats of algae growing on rocks and shells. Many scavengers live in this community, feeding upon locally produced waste material, or upon solid detritus settling among the mussels; such settling is facilitated by the shells' causing eddies as the water is swirled past them. Still another factor in such a community is a population of predators, feeding upon other animals and helping to control the population.

Eventually, every animal or plant must die, and the organic matter of its tissues is returned to the sea. This is done through the action of bacteria, which bring about the decomposition of dead bodies, or of the waste products from living ones, so allowing the all-important fertilizing trace elements to return to the water for further use.

Most marine communities are "open" systems, in which parts of the cycle occur outside the community itself. In our mussel bed, the energy-bearing planktonic plants may have drifted a great distance before arriving, and dead animals may be washed away from the community before they decompose. But somewhere in the sea the cycle is closed; the chain continues. And any creature of the sea or shore is not so much an entity in itself as it is a minute portion of a tremendous, continuous, world-wide process.

THE INTERTIDAL ZONE AS A PLACE TO LIVE

The narrow area between the normal limits of the tide, following thousands of miles of convoluted coastline, is perhaps the earth's most densely populated area. The millions of creatures living there have had to solve a number of problems in order to survive in a zone that is neither sea nor land, and that is

[24]

never quite the same from one moment to the next.

One such problem is that of wave shock. The intertidal zone is the chief focus of the surf, which brings tons of water crashing repeatedly against sand or rock. Well-attested accounts tell us something of the power in these breaking waves; in one instance, a stone weighing 80 tons was moved 70 feet across a rocky beach; and the windows of the lighthouse at Dunnet Head on the northern tip of Scotland, which are 290 feet above mean sea level, have repeatedly been broken by wave-hurled rocks. Where waves of this magnitude are frequent, of course, the rock surfaces may be scoured to barrenness, but where the forces are only a little less violent, there are many living things fully capable of withstanding them.

Perhaps the simplest way to resist the waves is to hide from them, and this is what hundreds of kinds of intertidal animals do; when the waves are dangerous, they crawl under or between stable rocks, and let these bear the brunt of the surf. Many animals spend their entire lives in such rocky retreats, often attached to the rocks, and never emerging even in periods of calm.

Rock-hiding is a good method, and a popular one; the intertidal collector finds many of his treasures by turning over loose stones. This is a good time to mention that the conscientious collector should always be very careful to replace every rock in its original position. If this is not done, a good collecting locality quickly presents a scene of devastation.

Sandy beaches are deficient in rocky hiding places, but the sand itself offers protection to burrowing animals. Such creatures as the pismo clam (*Tivela*) and the bean clam (*Donax*) live in this way, and can carry out all their life processes without the necessity of full emergence from the sand. Sand crabs (*Emerita*) are also burrowers, but they emerge from the sand after the main shock of each wave has passed, and swim

to a new locality. When the surf is running danger-
ously high, however, they retreat deeper into the sand
and stay there.

A beach covered with rounded pebbles or cobbles
offers neither the shelter of unmoving rocks nor the
possibility of deep burrowing, and such a beach is
relatively barren of marine life.

Starfish, limpets, and a number of other animals
crawl over the rocks when the waves are not too high;
when threatened with being swept away, however,
they stop moving and hang on tightly. Most of these
have low, rounded bodies or shells presenting a mini-
mum of resistance to the sweeping water.

Still other animals make a permanent attachment to
the rocks. Barnacles glue themselves down when they
are still in the larval form, and spend the rest of their
lives in that one spot. Mussels attach themselves by
"byssus" threads, each of which has its free end firmly attached to the substrate.

Seaweeds, too, are quite firmly attached to the
rocks, and like mussel beds, they provide a refuge for
a whole fauna. Dr. John Colman, studying the seaweed habitat on English shores, estimated that the
common lichen, *Lichina pygmaea*, contains among its
tufts an animal population approaching one million
individuals for each square meter of rock surface.

Permanent attachments of this sort constitute what
is known as a "sessile" way of life, and this would not
be possible on land, where an attached animal could
not get enough food. The moving waters of the sea,
however, carry a rich load of nourishing material, and
sessile animals have evolved many ways of collecting
this food. Barnacles, for example, have feathery legs,
which are swept rhythmically through the water,
straining out food particles. Mussels do not move
their nets through the water, but pump the water
through the nets; their gills act in this manner, serving
a double function as sieves and organs of respiration.

A large mussel filters as much as 16 gallons of water every day.

Some of the burrowing forms, such as the innkeeper (*Urechis caupo*) and the parchment worms (*Chaetopterus*), "spin" a sort of mucus net across their tunnels, then cause a current of water to flow through it. Later, the loaded nets are devoured, together with their contents. The tube snail, *Aletes*, also uses a mucus net, but it floats up in the water; a colony of these animals produces a community net, which is allowed to hang in the water for a while before being pulled in and eaten.

Selective digestion is used by the bloodworm (*Euzonus*) and many other forms. In the manner of the familiar earthworm, the bloodworm swallows large quantities of sand, passing it through the digestive tract while the digestive processes dissolve the contained food material. The lugworm, *Arenicola*, feeds in much the same manner, pushing aside about one-third of the sand in its path and swallowing the other two-thirds. If it is not hungry, the lugworm is able to burrow without swallowing any sand at all.

Beneath quiet waters, the ocean bottom is often covered by a film of organic debris, and this is used as food by many creatures. The bent-nosed clam, *Macoma nasuta*, buries itself in the sediments and exends its long, flexible incurrent siphon to the surface and above it; its tip bends down and just touches the food film, and acts as a vacuum cleaner in picking it up. Other animals use other methods to secure this detritus.

Seaweeds provide food to those relatively few animals capable of digesting it. Certain limpets feed upon the sea lettuce (*Ulva*) which grows upon rocks, and each limpet maintains its own personal grazing-ground like a well-kept lawn. Sea hares, abalones, and purple sea urchins eat just about any kind of seaweed.

[27]

Predation is a frequent means of procuring food. Such creatures as the octopus are skillful and active hunters. Even some of the sessile, permanently attached animals are predacious; sea anemones, for example, have tentacles armed with thousands of microscopic stinging cysts, with which they are able to capture and kill any small animal that blunders into them.

Active feeding of this sort usually goes on when the tide is high, so that water covers both predator and prey; during the periods of exposure to the air, the animals are generally quiescent. At these times, the animals are faced with the prospect of asphyxiation or desiccation, and many solutions to this problem have been evolved. Limpets and periwinkles attach themselves tightly to their rocky substrate, using their impermeable shells to slow down evaporative drying. Having no means of extracting oxygen from the air, they must literally hold their breath until the tide comes in.

The aggregate anemones keep their moisture intact through a process which may be explained by means of a principle of solid geometry. This is the principle that a large mass has relatively less surface area than a small mass of the same shape, and this has a pronounced effect upon drying. A single one of these anemones would have a very large surface area, through which evaporation would take place rapidly, in relation to its mass, but a whole host of them, crowded close together, act in some ways as a solid mass, with a correspondingly smaller ratio of exposed evaporative surface. These animals often occur in populations of 300 individuals per square foot of rock surface, and they are found in zones receiving much more air exposure than can be tolerated by the solitary anemones.

Animals sheltering under rocks, among mussels or seaweeds, or other ever-damp environments, have little trouble in maintaining their moisture. The sea-weeds themselves are somewhat protected by their numbers, and by their ability to sacrifice a few individual plants in order to protect the whole colony. The upper layers protect the lower ones, and while these upper parts may be damaged by the sun and the dry air, a reservoir of repair materials is kept going in the lower ones.

Barnacles and mussels simply close their shells together tightly whenever they are exposed to the air.

The reproduction of sessile animals—and of many mobile ones as well—is most often accomplished by external fertilization, in which eggs and sperm are separately discharged into the water. This is a wasteful method; many of the eggs are not fertilized, and those that are have no protection against being eaten, so that a large portion of the eggs never succeed in growing up. Survival is assured only by the production of tremendous numbers of eggs. Thus the eastern oyster produces some 500 million eggs every year, only one of which must attain maturity in order to perpetuate the species.

Where eggs and young are cared for by a parent, however, the chances of life go up, and such numbers are not necessary. A small Pacific coast fish known as the sarcastic fringehead (*Neoclinus blanchardi* Girard) illustrates this. The female lays only 300 or so eggs inside an old bottle or empty shell, and the zealously protective male stands guard over them until they hatch. Among the surfperches (family Embiotocidae) fertilization is internal and the young are born alive. These young are quite large, and can take fairly good care of themselves; each female has to produce only 10 to 25 young per year.

THE CLASSIFICATION OF ANIMALS

Man seems always to have felt the necessity of bestowing a name upon every living thing, and this, we

[29]

say, was one of the first jobs assigned to Adam. Adam's approach has been explained as his detecting a certain appropriateness in certain sounds; at least, Mark Twain quotes him as saying, in effect, "Well, it just *looks* like a buffalo, and that's what I'm going to call it!" And many names *do* possess a certain appropriateness, as witness Gracie Allen's remark at the circus: "Gosh, no wonder they call 'em 'elephants'—they're so big!"

But the sons of Adam have not shown much consistency in their naming. The same kind of animal has different names in different areas, and the same name may be used for several different — and unrelated — creatures. Furthermore, ordinary names do not usually convey any sense of relationship, and when they do, they're likely to be wrong. Names in the vernacular do not provide for the orderly arrangement of information, nor for any opportunity to make logical changes as the information improves. For these reasons, scientific names were invented.

Scientific names are bestowed only after a great deal of study, and the bestowal must follow many formal rules. These names are the same in every language, in every part of the world, and no two animals may have identical names; the first name correctly proposed is the official one; and so on. There are three codes of nomenclature, one each for botany, zoology, and bacteriology. Each of these is the product of an international congress of scientists, and together they constitute one of the oldest still-active instruments of international agreement.

A scientific name consists basically of two words, usually in Latinized Greek. The first word, always spelled with a capital initial letter, is known as the generic name, the name representing the genus. The second word, never with a capital initial (except when a botanist chooses to use a capital in a specific name derived from a proper noun) is the specific name, or

[30]

the name of the species. A species (note that the word is both singular and plural: the "s" is never dropped) in nature is considered as a population within which interbreeding is carried on, or is at least potentially possible; this population must be reproductively isolated from other populations. The genus is thought of as a group of related species, although there are many "monotypic" genera in which only one species is known. Unlike the species, the genus does not really represent a grouping that exists in nature, but is a purely man-made convenience.

A third name—the "subspecies"—may also form a part of the scientific name. This is indicative of a population that is different from neighboring groups, but with differences of a minor sort, usually showing a gradual intergradation. Two different subspecies could probably breed with each other, but are usually geographically isolated.

In technical writing, the authority, or author of the name, is indicated. Thus the full name of the California blind goby is written: *Typhlogobius californiensis* Steindacher; the authority is not italicized. After an author has set up a new name, it often happens that further research indicates a different relationship, and a species must be placed in a different genus. When a change of this sort happens, the name of the original author is retained, but is placed in parentheses: this is how it is with the name of the grunion, *Leuresthes tenuis* (Ayres).

The author of a new name must do more than merely "christen" his new creature; he must relate it to a whole hierarchy of classificatory groups which, although not part of the name itself, must be made known to biologists. Speaking in the simplest possible terms, these categorical groupings might be arrived at by a scientist who put all the kinds of plants and animals into a big pile, then started sorting them. First of all he would sort them into groups with very obvious differences, then would start sorting in more detail within each preliminary portion. After he had finished, right down to the smallest details that appeared important to him, he would have a framework of reference. If he didn't stop there, but continued his studies with increasing detail in the light of his increasing knowledge, he would find it necessary to shift some of his forms into other groups. For example, he might find that what he had thought to be basically similar characteristics were really only superficially similar, having gone through very different evolutionary and embryological processes; in other cases, he might find certain differences not as important as he had at first thought. In either case, his system of classification would have to allow for the making of such changes, as does the science of taxonomy today.

Although the position of a name within this framework may change, the framework itself remains stable in presenting a scheme of groups at various levels. The first big division is that of a Kingdom, which places a living object as an animal or a plant or as something else. (The old view was that there were only these two basic Kingdoms, but some authorities today prefer to name four Kingdoms: Monera, the blue-green algae and other non-nucleated forms; Protista, the dinoflagellates and other one-celled plant-like animals or animal-like plants; and the two big ones, Plantae and Animalia.) Each Kingdom is split up into a number of smaller groups, the Phyla (singular: Phylum). And so it goes: each Phylum is divided into Classes, each Class into Orders, each Order into Families, each Family into Genera, and each Genus into Species.

A number of intercategories may be used, and we frequently meet such terms as "Subphylum," "Superclass," "Suborder," and the like. In some groups, these categories assume quite a high importance; it would

[32]

be impossible, for example, to undertake a serious study of the classification of snails without frequent reference to Subgenera.

This scientific classification is, of course, a man-made thing, and is not a part of nature; it is an expression of our imperfect knowledge. Since the extent of our knowledge fortunately changes, the classification too must change. The scientific name is not a fixed, immovable entity. Taxonomists are in some ways like the first explorers in a strange land, who use whatever knowledge they have in applying names to geographical features. When later exploration shows that two different names have been given to different stretches of the same winding river, confusion will exist until everyone agrees to the dropping of one of the names. So don't be disturbed if the scientific names in one book are not the same as those in another; the whole process eventually leads to more precise classifications.

In regard to vernacular names, I have tried to be as consistent as possible in this book, and where several different names are acceptable, I have tried to choose the one doing the least violence to established relationships. But where a vernacular name has become firmly embedded in the language, there has been no attempt to call it "wrong" and change it: starfishes are called starfishes, even though they are in no way related to fishes—nor, for that matter, to stars.

A great temptation is to try to invest common names with more meaning than their framers intended. For example, the question often arises: "Is the California lobster 'really' a lobster? Isn't it 'really' a crayfish?" In this form, the question simply has no clear-cut answer. If enough people choose to call an animal "lobster," then lobster it is—even though it be not related to the Maine lobster. About all you can say is that in some parts of the world, these spiny lobsters are called crayfish. But it should be pointed out that they are

[33]

not at all closely related to the fresh-water crustaceans for which the term "crayfish" is widely accepted, and that the term is no more appropriate for one than it is for the other. Etymology doesn't help much in this instance, either; "crayfish" probably derives from the French "écrevisse," anything living in a crevice, and in this sense it could apply just as logically to the Maine lobster, although nobody seems to use it that way. The best thing is to listen to the natives, and call the spiny lobster "crayfish" in Florida, "lobster" in California, or "langouste" and "langosta" in French- and Spanish-speaking countries. Still better is the attainment of familiarity with the scientific name of the animal, *Panulirus interruptus* for the California species, and with its position in the hierarchy of scientific nomenclature.

Kingdom PROTISTA

Phylum MASTIGOPHORA

Class DINOFLAGELLATA

Although many kinds of one-celled creatures are tremendously important in the marine community, individual specimens are not to be seen without a microscope. Certain forms, however, do at times become so abundant as to be clearly observable, *en masse,* to the human eye—and often to the human nose as well. Chief among these are various members of the class Dinoflagellata, which are responsible for the periodic displays of the "red tide."

The Kingdom Protista was set up partly to account for this rather anomalous group, which cannot be clearly designated as either plant or animal. In terms of the general economy of the sea, however, there is little question: they function as plants. They possess chlorophyll, and use it in the carrying out of the pro-

[34]

cess of photosynthesis, thus acting as primary producers of organic matter.

The term "dinoflagellate" comes from two roots: the Latin "flagellum," meaning a little whip, and referring to the two whip-like organs of locomotion; and the Greek "dineo," meaning "to spin," in reference to the spiral progress through the water of the swimming organism.

Many species of dinoflagellates have the ability to produce light when they are disturbed, and when such species form the bulk of a red-water visitation, the surf on a moonless night presents a fireworks display that is never to be forgotten. A fish swimming through this water leaves a comet-like trail of luminescence in its wake, and fishermen used to find schools of sardines by watching for the telltale glow produced by a school swimming through the red water. Even after being cast up on the beach, these one-celled organisms continue their light-producing reaction to any disturbance; the feet of a beach-walker produce flashes of light each time they hit the wet sand, and a trail of slowly dimming footprints is left behind.

We don't know what purpose may be served by these light flashes, and those dinoflagellates that cannot produce them seem to get along as well as those that can. The chemical processes of the light production are somewhat better understood, but even here, a lot of work remains to be done. In nearly all luminescent life-forms, the light is produced by the interaction of a pair of chemicals, luciferin and luciferase. These two chemicals are found in the dinoflagellates but their operations are complicated by the presence of tiny crystalline particles called "scintillons." A change in the acidity of fluids surrounding the scintillons appears to be the triggering event, and it is somewhat mysterious just how luciferin and luciferase enter the picture.

A remarkable periodicity in the intensity of the

luminescence has recently been discovered. Dino-flagellates produce a brighter light during the night hours than they do during the day, and this is the case even if the organisms are kept in a completely dark laboratory. The brightest flashes occur at about 1:00 a.m., and the least light is produced around noon.

A common term for the light of the red-tide organisms is "phosphorescence," which is fine as long as one understands it in the original sense of the Greek words meaning "to bear light"; it has no connection with the chemical element, phosphorus. "Biolumi-nescence" is a less confusing term, and is preferred by biologists.

1. COMMON RED-TIDE ORGANISM—*Gonyaulax polyedra* Stein. This is one of our most abundant dinoflagellates, at times occurring in a concentration of 7 million cells per gallon of water. "Blooms" of this sort are most likely to come about during the warm late summer months, although there are instances of their having persisted through most of a year. This species is not, under ordinary circumstances, a poisonous one, but may occasionally constitute a danger to other forms of marine life. A large concentration may be moved into shallow water near shore, so that there are more cells than the water can support; after using up all the available oxygen, millions upon millions of the dino-flagellates die. Decay sets in, and the water becomes heavily contaminated with bacteria, and is then unfit for the support of fishes and other sea creatures. At such times, dead fish may be washed ashore in windrows.

Other kinds of dinoflagellates contain poisonous materials in their bodies, and may pollute the water even while themselves remaining alive. One of these is *Gymnodinium breve*, which periodically brings about destructive red tides on the coasts of Florida.

2. MUSSEL-POISON DINOFLAGELLATE—*Gonyaulax cate-nella* Whidon and Kofoid. This Pacific coast species

[36]

does not seem to produce any wholesale destruction of marine life, but it is quite capable of poisoning human beings. When this happens, it is not because the poison is ingested directly from the water; a swimmer can safely go among even the heaviest concentration, for he would have to swallow many gallons of sea water to take in enough cells to harm him. But if he were unfortunate enough to filter them out in some way, and swallow the concentrate, he would become very ill, and might even die; and this is exactly what can happen if he eats mussels during a period of this poisonous red water. Mussels are filter feeders, and the mussel-eater eats everything that the mussel has filtered from the water during the several preceding hours. There is danger not only from the undigested cells, but the poisonous materials from digested ones seem to be concentrated in certain parts of the mussel; this does not harm the mussel, but presents a grave danger to the human unlucky enough to eat it.

Gonyaulax catenella is extremely rare south of Point Conception, and there are no known cases of mussel-poisoning in Southern California. Nevertheless, this ailment is not one to be treated lightly, and one should never eat mussels anywhere on the Pacific Coast if there is the slightest possibility of their having been recently exposed to any kind of red water. Quarantine notices set up by local and State health departments, usually in the summer months, should be obeyed without question. Mussels are good to eat, but not good enough to risk your life for!

Cooking, by the way, does *not* destroy the toxin.

Clams are somewhat less dangerous than mussels, partly because we customarily discard the dark portions which contain the digestive organs; nevertheless, they should be eaten with caution during red-water seasons. Abalones, on the other hand, are not filter feeders, but grazers; they may be safely eaten at any time—subject, of course, to the game laws.

[37]

There are many hundreds of fascinating one-celled organisms to be found along our shores, but as they are not obvious to most beach visitors, they will not be discussed here.

Kingdom ANIMALIA

Phylum PORIFERA (The sponges)

Unlike the protists, the sponges are composed of many cells instead of a single cell; but unlike the higher animals, the sponge cells are assembled in a rather loose aggregation, and under some circumstances can carry on by themselves if separated from the whole group. A classic experiment showed that it was possible to squeeze a sponge gently through a piece of fine silk, so as completely to dissociate the cells, and have the cells not only survive but reassemble in the sponge form.

The word "porifera" means "pore-bearing," and refers to the numerous tiny openings scattered all over a sponge's body. These are incurrent openings, through which seawater flows inward, propelled by the beating of thousands of microscopic hair-like "cilia" lining the water passages and the inside of the body. Outgoing water, from which food particles and oxygen have been obtained, is channeled through different openings, which are larger and not so numerous. In many forms, there is only one of these excurrent openings, which is known as an "osculum." Water passing to the outside takes away waste metabolic products and, in the proper season, eggs and sperm.

All sponges have a "skeleton" composed of intertwined microscopic spicules, often of bizarre shapes. The material composing these spicules provides a primary criterion in sponge classification. In the class Calcarea, they are of calcium carbonate; in the class Hyalospongia (also known as Hexactinellida) they are of silicon, the material of which glass is made, and are usually of a six-sided shape; and in the class Demospongia the spicules are either of glass (in other than six-sided shapes) or a unique horny material called "spongin." The familiar bath sponge belongs to the class Demospongia, and the useful part consists of the spongin skeleton with all the flesh removed.

There are about 50 kinds of sponges along the California coast. Their accurate identification is a matter for a specialist equipped with a good microscope and lots of time. As a matter of fact, the primary identification of a specimen merely as a sponge is not always easy; many are irregular and inconsistent in shape, size, and color, and some of them resemble other kinds of unrelated animals. One general identifying mark is the presence of the hundreds of small pores, which often may not be seen except upon close scrutiny. Another feature is that most sponges have a gritty texture in contrast to some of the other superficially similar animals such as compound ascidians.

3. YELLOW SPONGE—*Mycale macginitiei* de Laubenfels. Forms thin, yellow, encrusting mats on the undersides of rocks, especially in quiet waters. An exception to the general rule about sponge surface texture, this one is fairly slick to the touch, although the presence of stiffening spicules is obvious.

4. SULPHUR SPONGE—*Verongia thiona* de Laubenfels. "Sulphur" is appropriate to both the color and the smell. It lives on the undersides of rocks, but makes thicker mats than the preceding species. This mat is composed of a number of fairly large individuals, and a raised osculum is seen in every three or four square inches of surface.

5. VANILLA SPONGE—*Xestospongia vanilla* de Laubenfels. Found all along the Pacific Coast. Forms a smooth, hard encrustation that looks like cake icing.

6. A RED SPONGE—*Plocamia karykina* de Laubenfels.

Color bright red. Forms mats of up to ¾ inches in thickness. The oscula are scattered irregularly over the surface (pl. 3c).

7. PURPLE SPONGE—*Haliclona permollis* Bowerbank. Very similar to no. 6, but is usually purplish, and its oscula are distributed in a regular pattern.

8. CRUMB-OF-BREAD SPONGE — *Halichondria panicea* (Pallas). These encrusting colonies are rarely more than an inch or so in diameter, but may be a quarter of an inch thick. Color orange or green—or almost any other color in between. While not abundant in Southern California, this is a cosmopolitan species, found in cool and temperate waters around the world. It was the subject of microscopic observation by the Scottish physician, R. E. Grant, who in 1825 watched the water currents flowing out of the oscula. Up to that time, naturalists had not agreed as to whether the sponge was a plant or an animal, although Aristotle had guessed at their animal relationships long before. The matter was settled by Dr. Grant's observations, and the sponges were recognized as animals.

9. FREE-LIVING SPONGE—*Tetilla mutabilis* de Laubenfels. Most sponges are firmly attached to some sort of substrate, but not this one; it lives on insubstantial mud flats. Young individuals are anchored to the mud by means of a holdfast of fibrous spicules, but those more than a couple of inches in length seem able to dispense with this security, and are moved about by tides and currents.

10. SKUNK SPONGE—*Lissodendoryx firma* (Lambe). Color yellow, surface formed into rounded lumps. These lumps are hollow, and furnish a home for many kinds of annelids, roundworms, and amphipods. When broken open, this sponge is found to have a rank and unpleasant odor. It is found on the underside of rocks, even those half buried in sand. More common in the northern part of our area.

11. PACIFIC LOGGERHEAD SPONGE — *Spheciospongia*

[40]

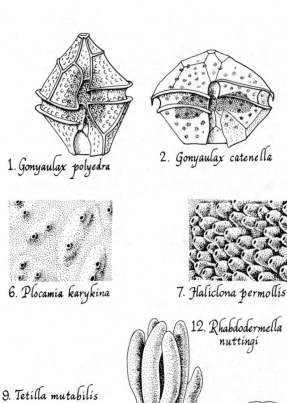

1. *Gonyaulax polyedra*

2. *Gonyaulax catenella*

6. *Plocamia karykina*

7. *Haliclona permollis*

12. *Rhabdodermella nuttingi*

9. *Tetilla mutabilis*

13. *Tethya aurantia*

confoederata de Laubenfels. The largest of our sponges, attaining the diameter of a bowling ball. Found at the extreme low tide level. It is not common, although it may be more abundant than it appears to be, for unless examined closely, it looks exactly like a round gray rock.

12. URN SPONGE—*Rhabdodermella nuttingi* Urban. Symmetrical, urn-shaped. Grows in clusters, suspended from crevice walls and overhanging rocks in the lowest tide zone. Each little pale gray urn may grow to a length of 2 inches or so. The urn shape is a common one among sponges, found in unrelated species all over the world.

13. ORANGE SPONGE — *Tethya aurantia* (Pallas). Round when viewed from the top, this sponge varies in profile from a slightly humped disk to a sphere. Diameter to 3 inches with a granular, lumpy surface of an orange color. It attaches itself to rocks, often in crevices, at the lowest tide level, and is fairly common. This is one of the many sponges having a great geographical and ecological range, found in most seas, from shallow shore waters to fairly great depths. It is an important part of the fauna attached to the walls of submarine canyons in California waters.

Phylum COELENTERATA (The jellyfishes and their relatives)

At first glance, the 9,000 species comprising this phylum make up an assemblage of bewilderingly different forms, but close examination shows these forms to be relatively superficial variations upon a central theme.

The basic plan of the coelenterates is a radial one, with a circle of tentacles surrounding a central mouth. The mouth, serving both for the ingestion of food and the ejection of wastes, opens directly into the body cavity, which does not contain a digestive tube, but itself constitutes the space where digestion takes place. (The name "coelenterate" comes from a combination of Greek words signifying "hollow" and "intestine.") The body is formed of two layers of cells, between which is sandwiched a gelatinous material called the "mesoglea."

A characteristic attribute of this phylum is the possession of tiny stinging structures known as "nematocysts"; these may occur upon any part of the body, but are usually most concentrated on the tentacles. They are tiny capsules containing a coiled line. A triggering mechanism, which appears to be operated by both chemical and mechanical stimuli, brings about a sudden increase of pressure within the capsule and violently ejects the free end of the line. This usually happens when an object bumps into the coelenterate, and the object is thereupon entangled in sticky threads or penetrated by poison-bearing harpoons, depending upon the type of nematocyst.

Most of the barbed nematocysts are too short to penetrate human skin, but this is not true in all species; some of the jellyfishes can inflict quite severe stings. The Portuguese man-of-war, which does not occur on this coast, is one of the most potent stingers, although one or two tropical species are even more virulent.

The exploding action is automatic on the part of the nematocyst, not depending upon any act of will of the animal. For this reason, a dead jellyfish may, if handled, sting as badly as a living one, and fishermen using hand lines have often been stung by their lines after they have been dragged through a school of jellyfish, picking up some nematocysts in the process. These stinging structures are used for protection and for food-getting, and, in some cases, for locomotion. Each nematocyst operates only once, and then must be replaced.

The phylum Coelenterata is divided into three classes: Hydrozoa (hydroids and related forms), Scyphozoa (the large "true" jellyfishes), and Anthozoa (the sea anemones, corals, and related forms).

Class HYDROZOA

The hydroids are usually quite plant-like in appearance. They may occur as solitary polyps, but are more often found in colonies; some kinds form a barely visible "fuzz" on the surface of a rock or a piece of seaweed, and other kinds grow as bushes several inches high. Perhaps the largest hydroid is a solitary one, *Branchiocerianthus*, a fragile animal living in the quiet waters at a depth of 15,000 feet; it is 8 feet high. There are a great many kinds in the area covered by this book, and only a few of these can be considered here.

14. BROWN BUSHY HYDROID — *Eudendrium californicum* Torrey. Grows in brown, 6-inch seaweed-like clusters in rocky tide pools in the extreme low tide zone. As in most hydroids, the polyps are easily visible through a good hand lens. The colony is spirally formed around stiff branching stems of a brown color. The individual polyps are pink, with white tentacles.

A feature of most hydroid colonies, including this one, is the assignment of special jobs to specialized individual polyps; some are responsible for collecting food, while others are in charge of breeding. In this species, the breeding polyps produce tiny jellyfish-like medusae, which remain fixed to the parent colony. (In many hydroids, as we shall see later, the medusae are set free to swim away and reproduce elsewhere.) The whole colony is united by a single digestive tract, so that whatever is eaten by one member supplies nutriment to all. An individual polyp could not survive if detached from the colony; in fact, the term "individual" has hardly any meaning when applied to colonial animals of this sort.

15. SOLITARY HYDROID—*Corymorpha palma* Torrey. Length to 4 inches. Color yellowish, almost transpar-

ACTUAL SIZE →

14
Eudendrium californicum

15
Corymorpha palma

16
Tubularia crocea

17
Clytia bakeri

18
Obelia dichotoma

19
Abietinaria greenei

20
Aglaophenia struthionides

21
Plumularia setacea

ent. Very much resembles an elongated sea anemone. Found on mud flats, from the middle low tide zone downward. While under water, this hydroid stands upright, with the root-like processes at the lower end of its stalk firmly embedded in the mud. At times of low tide, when exposed to the air, the animal collapses, lying flaccidly at the surface. It has two basic ways of feeding. When a current of water is flowing past, it remains motionless in an upright position, allowing the moving water to deposit food upon its tentacles. When the water is not flowing, however, it makes repeated bowing motions in different directions, bending down and brushing the tentacles across the surface of the mud.

This solitary hydroid is common wherever you can find a good mud flat; such spots are, however, increasingly rare, and the whole habitat is in grave danger of disappearing under the avalanche of seaside "improvement." California once had at least 382,000 estuarine acres, but 256,000 acres (67 percent of the total) have been destroyed. It is devoutly to be hoped legislation will save examples of this habitat.

16. OATEN-PIPE HYDROID—*Tubularia crocea* (Agassiz). Stems to 5 inches long, rarely branched. Grows in large clumps attached to pier pilings in quiet water, at the lowest tide level. Some of the stalks are longer than others, extending beyond the bulk of the clump; each of these long stalks bears a pinkish polyp at the tip. The polyps have two circlets of tentacles, between which lie grape-like clusters of medusoids, which comprise the medusa stage of the species. The medusae are not set free, but remain attached to the hydranth (another term for polyp) until their first circlet of tentacles has grown and they are ready to settle down on their own.

Because of their ability to regenerate lost parts, the hydroids have been the subject of much study, and the various species of *Tubularia* (there are about 14, with worldwide distribution) have received the most attention. The hydranths are ready to drop off at a moment's notice, as when the water becomes stale or warm; when conditions improve, new heads are regenerated on the old stalks, and under some circumstances, a discarded hydranth will grow a new stalk.

17. CLAM HYDROID—*Clytia bakeri* Torrey. Length to ½ inch. This little hydroid grows attached to the shell of the bean clam, *Donax gouldii*, or to that of the pismo clam, *Tivela stultorum*. Both of these clams inhabit surf-swept beaches, and bury themselves in the sand; the hydroid is located so that even though the clam is below the surface of the sand, most of the hydroid's length extends up into the overlying water.

There are about 27 species of *Clytia* in North America. The genus is quite closely related to *Obelia*, which will be discussed in succeeding paragraphs.

18. BRANCHED OBELIA — *Obelia dichotoma* (Linn). Length about 1 inch, colonies forming an inch-thick mat on all sorts of objects submerged in sea water. Common all along the Pacific coast in the low tide zone. *Obelia* belongs to the great group of sheathed hydroids, with each feeding polyp growing inside a transparent cup into which the polyp may be retracted. The reproductive polyps are borne in urn-shaped cups set at the angles of the branches. These urns release tiny medusae, about 1 millimeter (1/30 in.) in diameter; representing the sexual stage of the life cycle, these medusae swim away and produce larvae which settle down and grow up as the fixed stage. In another species, this whole process of alternating generations, from one medusa stage through the fixed stage to the next medusa stage, has been observed to take place in one month.

There is an almost worldwide distribution of the genus *Obelia*, with at least 26 known species. A number of these, all quite similar to this species, occur in Southern California.

[47]

19. FERN HYDROID — *Abietinaria greenei* Murray. Length to 1 inch. Fronds rather fern-like. This is one of the most widespread of our hydroids, found from the Queen Charlotte Islands south to Bahia San Quintín in Baja California. It is found most often attached to rocks in the lowest part of the intertidal zone, and has been observed by divers at depths to 200 feet. The transparent polyps are contained in cups set directly on the branch, without the slender connecting stem of the preceding species.

20. OSTRICH-PLUME HYDROID—*Aglaophenia struthionides* (Murray). Length to 4 or 5 inches. Color usually dark brown. In shape, very much like a feather. This species attaches to various sorts of substrate, often in clusters of a score or more of the feathery branches, and is rather often found washed up on the shore without any attachment at all.

Some of the branchlets of the "feather" are much thicker than the others; these are known as "corbulae," and they contain the sexual generation, which is not set free in a medusa form, but retained until they produce eggs. These eggs produce tiny ciliated larvae, which are set free; they settle down nearby and grow up into the ostrich-plume form.

21. GLASSY PLUME HYDROID—*Plumularia setacea* (Ellis). Length ½ inch. Transparent, and, in usual light, almost invisible. Found on many substrates, but easiest to see in our area as a fuzzy growth on the stipe and bulbs of cast-up kelp.

Like its relative, the ostrich-plume hydroid, this species does not release its medusae, but retains them in a sac until they produce larvae ready to assume the hydroid form. This method of reproduction is common among hydroids living in wave-pounded rocky areas, and apparently constitutes a positive adaptation to this rugged environment: delicate free-swimming medusae would be battered to bits before they could reach a quiet spot.

22. PURPLE SAILING JELLYFISH — *Velella velella* (Linnaeus). Diameter about 4 inches; color usually purple-blue on the edges, clear and transparent in the center and the sail. This is a high-seas species which does not belong on the beach, and their occasional presence in vast numbers is the result of some sort of hydrographic accident.

In the open sea, *Velella* often covers literally acres of the sea surface. Every few years, some quirk of wind or current, or both, drives them to their death ashore. The process inevitably damages them, rubbing away much of the delicate blue "skin" which covers the entire body of the healthy animals.

Although many older books describe *Velella* as a co-operating colony of polyps of varied form and function, recent observation has shown that it is really an individual animal, very similar to the polyps of hydroids such as *Corymorpha*. It is thus now placed in a group of hydroids known as the Chondrophora, rather than among the Siphonophores as formerly.

A conspicuous feature of *Velella* is the little sail, made of what appears to be clear plastic sheeting and set obliquely across the oval body. The sail and the float, made of gas-filled tubes bent into concentric rings, are more resistant to decay than the rest of the body, and may remain on the beach long after all the purple portions have disappeared. They are of such light construction that the wind has been known to carry them several miles inland.

Velella is thoroughly equipped with nematocysts, and some humans are reported to have been mildly stung by them, although I have handled thousands of them without injury.

Class SCYPHOZOA (The "true" jellyfishes)

23. PURPLE-STRIPED JELLYFISH — *Pelagia noctiluca* (Forskål). Diameter of the bell to at least 5 feet, and tentacles to a length of more than 20 feet. Such giants

[49]

are not at all common, however, and most specimens washed ashore are about 1 foot in diameter.

Like *Velella,* this species is at home in the open ocean, but beached specimens are quite common during the summer months. It is very fragile, and most of these specimens have been damaged by their passage through the surf.

The nematocysts of *Pelagia* are quite capable of penetrating human skin, and it is thus one of the most potent stingers of California waters. Even small pieces of the dead animal retain their stinging capacity, and handling or stepping upon fragments may produce a temporary burning rash. The most serious stings are those inflicted upon bathers who get tangled in the long, almost invisible trailing tentacles. Some people are allergically sensitive to the poison injected by the nematocysts, and show a very strong reaction. This is not common, however, and the sting is usually nothing to worry about for more than a few minutes, especially if the afflicted area can be washed with ammonia.

Many of the larger kinds of jellyfishes are accompanied by small fishes, making their home with apparent impunity among the stinging tentacles, and *Pelagia* is no exception. Its consorts in Southern California may be juvenile yellowfin or spotfin croakers, both of which have a habit of congregating about almost any floating object. How they keep from getting stung is a mystery.

Class ANTHOZOA (Sea anemones and their relatives)

24. SEA PANSY—*Renilla köllikeri* Pfeffer. Diameter 2½ inches, color purple. The sea pansy is most likely to be seen in the extreme low tide zone in muddy or sandy bays, although they are also abundant in the sandy bottoms of deeper water beyond the breakers. The purple disc-shaped body is usually buried in the

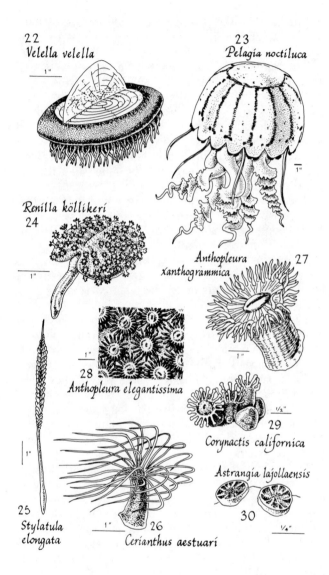

22
Velella velella

1"

23
Pelagia noctiluca

1"

Renilla köllikeri
24

1"

Anthopleura
xanthogrammica   27

1"

28
Anthopleura elegantissima

1"

Corynactis californica
29

1/2"

Astrangia lajollaensis

30

1/4"

25
Stylatula
elongata

1"

26
Cerianthus aestuari

1"

[51]

substrate, with the polyps protruding upward into the water; the stalk turns downward, apparently functioning as an anchor.

The tentacles of the polyps have nematocysts, and they capture and ingest any small bits of food that bump into them. The colony also uses a second method of feeding: a mucus net is secreted and held up by the polyps, and when it becomes full of entrapped particles, the net is swallowed.

The sea pansy is brilliantly luminescent under certain conditions, in a manner very much like that of the sea pen, no. 25.

The preferred habitat of the sea pansy is rapidly disappearing, and intertidal specimens are hard to find. People who can dive to 25 or 30 feet, however, can count on seeing plenty of them.

25. SLENDER SEA PEN—*Stylatula elongata* (Gabb). This form too requires quiet waters, and is most often seen in the mud flats or on the open coasts at depths of 50 feet or more.

The sea pen is supported by a central limy axis, around which cluster a great many polyp-bearing "leaves." The whole animal is attached to a bulb which is buried in the substrate; at low tide, when the soft parts would otherwise be exposed, they slide down the axis and huddle in the mud, leaving only an inch or two of the central stalk sticking out. When the tide is in, the stalk is pushed up so that a good portion of its 10-inch length is in the water, and the soft parts are expanded so as almost to cover it.

The sea pen is noted for its light-producing abilities. Flashes are produced when the polyps are prodded or otherwise disturbed, especially if the animal has been kept in the dark for a few preceding hours. If the body is touched at the midpoint, waves of light will travel in both directions away from the point of stimulation. A stimulus at one end, however, will cause the wave of light to travel in only one direction.

These waves are produced by the lighting in turn of individual polyps, and grow dimmer as they move away from the point of stimulation. If the disturbance is produced at two points simultaneously, two light waves will move toward one another, and where they meet and overlap, the light will be brighter.

There are many kinds of sea pens, but most of the others are confined to deep water.

26. TUBE-BUILDING ANEMONE — *Cerianthus aesturi* Torrey and Kleeberger. Tentacle-spread 4 to 5 inches. Fairly common, but, because of its retiring habits, not often seen; this is a burrowing form, and it constructs a long tunnel lined with mucus, in which are embedded a great many detached—but still operable— nematocysts. These burrows have been reported as reaching a length of 6 feet, but this is quite unusual.

This species has two rings of tentacles—a short set right around the mouth and a long, slender set located peripherally. These tentacles are expanded at the mouth of the burrow, and, upon being retracted, drag through the mud leaving a characteristic star-shaped track.

27. SOLITARY GREEN ANEMONE—*Anthopleura xanthogrammica* (Brandt). Diameter, including tentacles, to 10 inches, although 4 or 5 inches is more usual. Color variable; specimens in exposed situations usually bright green. This is one of our most abundant and most spectacular anemones. Its favorite habitat consists of rocks embedded in sand; the anemone may appear to be attached to the sand itself, but if its stalk is followed far enough, it will be found to be attached to a rock. The brilliant green of the disc and tentacles is due to the presence in the tissues of a kind of one-celled alga; these tiny plants cannot live in the absence of sunlight, which is why the green color is not seen in anemones living in the shade.

Any small object touching the tentacles is instantly penetrated by scores of toxic nematocysts, and held in place. The tentacles are then curved so as to point toward the mouth, while the rhythmic beating of microscopic cilia moves the object along until it drops into the mouth. Digestion is very rapid, and indigestible portions are ejected in an amazingly short time.

The nematocysts are too short to go through human skin, and the tentacles may be touched without harm. Some daring people have reported that the skin of the tongue is thinner, and touching this organ to the anemone can cause a tingling sensation. I have not tried this.

If they can be removed from their subtrate without injury to the base, these anemones will live well in the home seawater aquarium; several of them thrived for more than 30 years in the public aquarium at the Scripps Institution of Oceanography, while a related species in Scotland lived for over 70 years in captivity (pl. 4c).

28. AGGREGATE ANEMONE—*Anthopleura elegantissima* (Brandt). Very much like the preceding species, but much smaller, rarely exceeding an expanded diameter of 2 or 3 inches. It is extremely abundant in the upper parts of the middle tide zone, forming a dense mat completely covering large areas of rock—especially the steep rock faces on the side facing the sea. When the tide is out, each anemone folds in upon itself, forming a flattened sphere; since the surface of the column is covered with bits of shell and gravel, these retracted colonies look like the rock itself, and many a beach visitor is dismayed to find that he is stepping not upon solid stone, but upon the yielding bodies of hundreds of aggregate anemones.

A major means of reproduction in this species is by means of fission, a process which produces two individuals of the same sex. Within a given area, the members of an aggregation will thus be either all male or all female, permitting speculation that a single individual gave rise to the whole community. A patch of females may be next to a patch of males, although the former appear to be the more abundant.

Occasionally a colony may be found in a tide pool, where they may be observed in the expanded state; the delicate precision of their radial shape and the varicolored bands on the tentacles present a beautiful sight indeed, and the specific name *elegantissima* is seen to be an apt one (pls. 4*a,b*).

29. PINK ANEMONE—*Corynactis californica* Carlgren. Diameter 1 inch or less. Occasionally seen, in Southern California, on pier pilings at extreme low tide. May be identified by its small size, red or pink color, and the white knobbed tentacles. Like many marine animals, this one has a range apparently governed largely by water temperature; in the northern parts of its range, it lives well up in the intertidal zone. Toward the south, it makes its home at progressively greater depths, thus keeping in water of roughly the same temperature. In Southern California, one may find colonies as large as those near Puget Sound, but they are at a depth of 30 feet or more.

30. SOLITARY CORAL—*Astrangia lajollaensis* Durham. The deposition of lime in sufficient quantities to form a coral reef is a process requiring water warmer than ours, and there are no reef-forming corals on the California coast. There are, however, several kinds of solitary corals, of which this is the most abundant species. It is often found attached to solid objects in deeper water, but it also grows on rocks in the intertidal zone, although there the growth of small seaweeds and other organisms makes it hard to find. The polyps, when fully expanded, are about 1 inch in diameter, and each one has its separate "cup," about ¼ inch across. The radiating septa of these cups are typical of the corals in general.

Phylum CTENOPHORA (The comb jellies)
No ctenophores live in the intertidal zone, but at

least one species is rather frequently washed ashore. The ctenophores are not umbrella-shaped like most jellyfishes, but are either nearly spherical or very much elongated. Swimming is accomplished by means of eight columns of comb-like bristles ("ctenophore" means "comb-bearing"), whose rhythmic waving motions propel the animal. There are only two tentacles, and these are retractable into a tentacle sheath. Most species are brilliantly luminescent.

31. SEA GOOSEBERRY—*Pleurobrachia bachei* A. Agassiz. Diameter ½ inch. These little crystal-clear spheres are sometimes seen on the beach after a storm. Their native habitat is the open ocean, where their exceptional transparency makes them almost completely invisible. Sometimes the beach-stranded specimens are relatively unharmed, and will begin swimming about if placed in a jar of clean seawater.

Phylum PLATYHELMINTHES (The flatworms)

There are three classes in this phylum. Two of these, the flukes (Trematoda) and the tapeworms (Cestoda), are parasitic, and we will not consider them here. The other class, Turbellaria, has a few parasites in its ranks, but most members are free-living, and many of these are marine.

In the animals considered to this point, the basic plan of symmetry has been a radial one, symmetrical around a center point. The flatworms, however—and most of the groups to be considered hereafter, except for the starfishes—are bilaterally symmetrical, with a right side and left side which are mirror images of each other. Flatworms, unlike the jellyfishes, have layers of tissue between the two dermal layers, and these inner parts may consist of muscle, reproductive organs, and connecting tissue. There is only one opening to the digestive tract (although some species have *no* digestive tract) serving both as mouth and anus.

The free-living turbellarians have microscopic cilia

covering the outer surface of the body. The beating of these cilia creates a disturbance—a turbulence—in the water, which is where the class gets its name. All are carnivorous, and all obtain their food through a process of turning the throat inside out through the mouth, which is located near the center of the body's lower surface.

The members of this class are retiring in habit, living among rocks and seaweeds in our area. None is more than a couple of inches in length. The turbellarian fauna of Southern California has not been studied in great detail, and some of our forms have not been named; accurate identification is thus not really possible at this point.

32. COMMON FLATWORM — *Leptoplana acticola* Boone. Length ½ inch. Color tan or gray, but somewhat translucent, and so taking on the color of the substrate. Very common on the undersides of rocks in the middle and lower tide zones. When a sheltering rock is turned over, these flatworms will often be seen moving along it very much ". . . as a drop of glycerine flows down the sides of a glass dish," to use the words of Edward F. Ricketts.

33. FUZZY FLATWORM — *Thysanozoon* (species unknown.) Length to 1½ inches. Back covered with many small brown or gray papillae, giving the appearance of coarse fur. Much firmer in texture than the preceding species. Fairly common in the middle and lower tide zones in rocky areas. If removed from its rock and set free in the water, this flatworm swims gracefully and well, with a characteristic waving motion of the edges of its flat body.

Phylum NEMERTEA (The proboscis worms or ribbon worms)

This is another group whose retiring habits make its members almost unknown to most of us. This is somewhat surprising in the light of the size attained

[57]

by some; at least one species is reliably reported to reach a length of 75 feet! They are extremely flexible and ductile animals, able to thicken the body and contract it to a fraction of its maximum length.

Ribbon worms are unique in the possession of a certain type of eversible proboscis—a "nose" than can be turned inside out. This organ lies in a sort of sheath above the mouth. In some species, its tip is armed with hooked stylets, while in others, it is covered with a sticky mucus. In either instance, the proboscis is used for the capture of food. Most nemerteans are burrowers, spending their active hours crawling through tunnels either of their own devising or made by other creatures. Their long proboscises, which may be as long as the body, are continually sent scouting the burrows ahead of the main body of the ribbon worm, ready to subdue and retrieve annelid worms or other food.

Collection of certain kinds of ribbon worms in a whole state is practically impossible, for they very readily autotomize—that is, they break themselves into pieces if disturbed. Each piece thus produced may regenerate the parts necessary to become a whole animal. The late Dr. Wesley R. Coe found that any piece of *Lineus vegetus* which was not less in length than one-half its diameter would regenerate, and become a whole animal in 3 to 4 weeks. He speculated that this might constitute a major mode of reproduction in this and other species.

34. PINK NEMERTEAN—*Procephalothrix major* (Coe). Length (rarely) to 4 feet; diameter of body to 1/16 inch. Color ranges from light straw to deep pink, with anterior portion usually darker than posterior. In sand or clay under rocks in the low tide zone; the thread-like body is usually snarled into tangled knots not spiralled into coils.

35. BANDED NEMERTEAN — *Lineus vegetus* Coe. Length 6 inches. Color, olive or red-brown, lighter

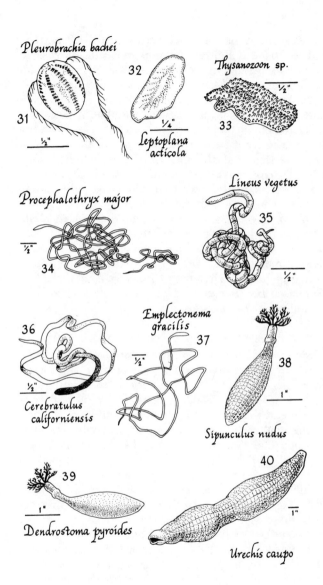

Pleurobrachia bachei

31

½"

32

¼"

Leptoplana
acticola

Thysanozoon sp.

½"

33

Procephalothryx major

½"

34

Lineus vegetus

35

½"

36

½"

Cerebratulus
californiensis

Emplectonema
gracilis

37

½"

38

1"

Sipunculus nudus

39

1"

Dendrostoma pyroides

40

1"

Urechis caupo

beneath; body usually encircled by up to 20 narrow, lighter bands. Fairly common beneath stones, in crevices, and among coralline seaweeds in the middle tide zone, and is also found in muddy areas.

36. FRAGILE NEMERTEAN—*Cerebratulus californiensis* Coe. Length to 10 inches. Very variable in color, usually matching the substrate; head often darker than body. The front part of the body is usually round in cross section, but the hinder part is flattened to a ribbon shape. Living in muddy or sandy bottoms in quiet waters, at the lowest intertidal level, this is one of our commonest nemerteans.

37. GREEN NEMERTEAN — *Emplectonema gracile* (Johnston). Length to 20 inches, diameter about 1/16 inch. Color green, lighter below. Fairly common among mussel beds. The best identifying description is that of Joel W. Hedgpeth (*Seashore Life of the San Francisco Bay Region*): it looks like "sticky bootlaces strung about the mussels."

Phylum SIPUNCULOIDEA (The peanut worms)

Sipunculid worms were first mentioned in scientific literature about 400 years ago, and ever since then there has been much uncertainty as to their proper taxonomic position. Today, however, most zoologists are agreed that the group should constitute a phylum.

Sipunculids live in great variety of habitats, from the intertidal zone to abyssal depths of at least 3 miles. Most of the 250 species, however, are confined to shallow shore waters, and all are marine.

At the anterior end of the body there is a retractable ring of branched, tree-like tentacles. Upon retraction, these tentacles are turned outside in, as it were, and together with the forward one-third of the body are folded into the larger posterior two-thirds. In this retracted position, some species somewhat resemble the kernel of a peanut. The shape and arrangement of the tentacles, together with the number of bands of retracting muscles, provide major features for use in classification. There are probably a dozen species in our area, but two of these will serve to illustrate the major characteristics of the group.

38. WHITE PEANUT WORM — *Sipunculus nudus* Linnaeus. Length occasionally to 10 inches, although most individuals are very much smaller, with 3 or 4 inches being average. Color shiny, iridescent white, and the surface is composed of small rectangular "bumps" arranged in orderly ranks and rows. Found in quiet waters with sandy bottoms. The animal feeds by swallowing the copious quantities of sand which adhere to its sticky tentacles; any edible matter among the swallowed sand is digested, while the sand itself is passed on through. In this manner, *Sipunculus* plays an important earthworm-like role in the conditioning of sandy bay and estuarine beaches. This species is widely distributed, known in tropical and temperate areas of the Pacific, Atlantic, and Indian Oceans, and in the Mediterranean and Adriatic Seas.

39. TAN PEANUT WORM — *Dendrostoma pyroides* Chamberlin. Length usually 3 or 4 inches, although 8-inch giants have been collected in northern California. Color usually pale tan or straw; body covered with very small tubercles, giving a felt-like texture. Often found under small rocks embedded in the sand of exposed beaches, usually at middle or low tide level. When placed in a jar of clean sea water, the animal will usually expose its finely branched tentacles.

Phylum ECHIUROIDEA (The echiuroid worms)

There are only about 60 species in this phylum, all living in shallow coastal waters. Several species are found on the Pacific Coast.

40. INNKEEPER — *Urechis caupo* Fisher and MacGinitie. Length 8 to 18 inches. Flesh-colored. Found in mud flats all along the California coast; in Southern

California, it seems to be most abundant in Newport Bay.

The innkeeper lives in a U-shaped burrow, the ends of which are at the surface of the mud and about 16 inches to 3 feet apart. The animal crawls forward in this permanent tunnel, and attaches a ring of slime to its walls; this forms the beginning of a slime net, which is spun out as the animal crawls backward. It thus forms a funnel-shaped net of mucus, about 8 inches long, and no water can flow through the burrow without passing through the net. The innkeeper's body is of sufficient diameter nearly to fill the tunnel, and rhythmic peristaltic motions create an effective flow of water through it. The net has extremely fine openings, so that all particles larger than about 4 millionths of an inch are filtered out of the flowing water. When the net has become clogged and the pumping difficult, the innkeeper crawls forward again, this time swallowing the net and its contents *en route*. It actually swallows only the smaller particles, and pushes the larger ones aside; these provide food to the numerous worms, clams, crabs, and fishes which share the innkeeper's burrow and give it its name.

Phylum ANNELIDA (The annelid worms)

The common earthworm is the most familiar member of this phylum. There are about 7,000 other species, divided into classes including the leeches, the earthworms, and the bristle worms or polychaetes; the polychaetes are the most numerous by far, and are typical of marine waters. There are also two other small classes, Archiannelida and Myzostomida, but these will not be discussed here.

The word "Annelida" is taken from a root meaning "ringed," in reference to the ring-like body segments. For the most part, each annelid segment is quite a bit like the two segments on either side of it, and one finds very few sudden "changes" as he looks along the length of one of these creatures.

The class Polychaeta has been divided into two groups called Errantia and Sedentaria, the names referring to the wandering habits of most of the Errantia and the sedentary habits of the typical members of the Sedentaria. Although there are some physical features consistent with this behavioral classification, the terms have little evolutionary significance, and are falling out of favor.

Each segment of a typical polychaete worm is equipped with a pair of bundles of bristles ("Polychaeta" means "many bristles") protruding from footlike organs known as parapodia. In most swimming polychaetes, and some of the sedentary ones as well, a part of the parapodium is extended so as to form a sort of paddle, supported by stiff bristles set at right angles to the body.

There are polychaetes adapted to every type of marine environment in every climate; some species are widely distributed, while others are quite local. There are about 650 known species from Pacific shores, about 550 of which are confined to the coasts of Oregon and Washington.

As with so many of the abundant marine invertebrates, the annelids are not easily identified by the layman; even the specialist cannot depend upon field identification, but must take his specimens to the laboratory for extremely detailed examination. Accordingly, only a few of the more obvious kinds will be mentioned here.

41. SCALE WORM — *Halosydna johnsoni* (Darboux). Length ½ inch, occasionally longer. Color pale brown, with white centers in the scales, which lie in two longitudinal rows of overlapping plates. Found in a variety of habitats, most often seen at the middle tide level on rocky shores. Some individuals live a free life, wandering among the rocks and crevices, while others take up a more sedentary existence as unin-

vited residents in the burrow of some other creature. The sedentary individuals are the larger and more brightly colored.

This species carries its fertilized eggs cemented to the body beneath the shielding scales. The young move away in the form of "trochophore" larvae; these soon sink to the bottom, there to grow into the adult stage.

42. PILEWORM — *Neanthes succinea* (Frey and Leuckart). Length to 18 inches, although the average is much smaller. This animal is capable of living under a wide variety of conditions, and lives not only in many sorts of marine habitats all along the Pacific coast, but is abundant in the inland Salton Sea, and has even been found in the waters of Oakland's Lake Merritt. The Salton Sea population is the result of deliberate importation; it forms an important link in the food chain involving the orange-mouth corbina, a popular sportfish which was also artificially introduced.

The pileworm makes excellent fish bait, and is sold in bait stores for this purpose. In looks and habits, it is much like the clam worm, *Nereis vexillosa*, no. 43.

43. CLAM WORM—*Nereis vexillosa* Grube. Length to 3 feet; in fact, there is a report of a 6-footer (possibly another, but closely related, species) found at Catalina Island. Most individuals are a great deal smaller, but even an 18-inch specimen is a magnificent creature, far indeed from the lowly thing brought to mind by the metaphorical use of the word "worm."

The color is olive or blue-green, often strikingly iridescent.

Nereis, like many polychaetes, is a predator, eating all manner of small creatures; it also eats the sea lettuce, *Ulva*.

The breeding cycle of many members of this group of worms is rather spectacular. At the breeding season, both sexes undergo a number of changes in their body

[64]

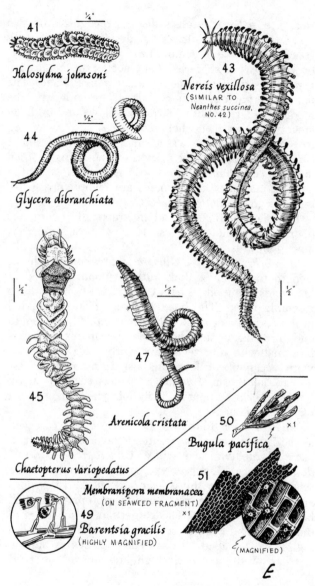

41 ¼"
Halosydna johnsoni

43
Nereis vexillosa
(SIMILAR TO
Neanthes succinea,
NO.42)

44 ½"
Glycera dibranchiata

½"

½"

½"

45
Chaetopterus variopedatus

47
Arenicola cristata

50
Bugula pacifica
×1

51
Membranipora membranacea
(ON SEAWEED FRAGMENT)
×1

49
Barentsia gracilis
(HIGHLY MAGNIFIED)

(MAGNIFIED)

E

[65]

structure; early naturalists did not recognize the two forms as different phases in the life of the same species, and the breeding form was named *Heteronereis,* a word still used (but not as the name of a genus) to designate the sexually active stage. The male heteronereis, at some "signal" provided by the moon-phase and tide, joins his fellows in suddenly emerging from their sheltered places and swimming to the surface of the water; there they thrash about furiously, shedding their sperm. The females then join this eerie ballet while releasing their eggs. At the conclusion, males and females are completely spent, and sink to the bottom in death.

The clam worm is found in practically every sort of marine habitat, but is perhaps most numerous among mussels.

44. BLOODWORM – *Glycera dibranchiata* Ehlers. Length to 8 inches. Body rather smooth, tapered at both ends, parapodia small. Color reddish; body fluids resemble blood. The head contains a large infolded proboscis, which can be instantly extended to a length one-third that of the body. The end of this proboscis is armed with four teeth, and with these the bloodworm is capable of delivering a sharp nip to a careless human hand; a mild venom is associated with such a bite, and brings about an irritation which may persist for several hours.

This species is found on the Atlantic Coast as well as the Pacific, and in every area is favored as fish bait.

45. PARCHMENT TUBE WORM—*Chaetopterus variopedatus* (Renier). Length occasionally to 15 inches. The scientific name of this species means "bristle-wing" and "various kinds of feet," and is appropriate, as will be seen in a moment. The vernacular name refers to the fact that the worm secretes a parchment-like lining for its U-shaped burrow. The ends of this burrow are narrowed, and project slightly above the mud floor.

rock, but it regularly leaves its home in order to graze nearby, returning at daylight (pl. 6a).

54. CONSPICUOUS CHITON — *Stenoplax conspicua* (Carpenter). Length to 6 inches. Color gray and brown, usually with pink in centers of the valves. This is our largest local chiton. It is most often found on the undersides of small, rounded rocks that are half-buried in the sand of the outer beaches. When such a rock is turned over, the conspicuous chitons attached to it will crawl toward the darkness with surprising speed.

Class GASTROPODA (The snails)

The snails constitute one of the more numerous groups of animals, about 65,000 kinds having been recognized. They are sometimes known as "univalves," since each has a single shell. These shells in every case start out in a spiral form, but in some groups, such as the limpets, the spiral shape is not discernible in the adults.

There are at least 300 kinds of snails within the geographic area covered by this book, and their accurate identification requires detail not possible here. In fact, some groups have not been taxonomically studied in recent years, and much work remains to be done in the classification of their relationships.

THE LIMPETS. These are snails whose shells are of a simple shield or plate shape, showing none of the usual spiral construction; in fact, some families have carried the conical shape so far that spiraling is not discernible even in the youngest stages. Limpets live on rocks, seaweeds, pier pilings, and other types of substrate, and are entirely herbivorous. The inside of the shell is never iridescent.

55. SHIELD LIMPET—*Acmaea pelta* Eschscholtz. Diameter 1 inch. Shape oval, conical, with point of cone well off-center toward the front. Color gray or cream, with interrupted radial stripes of black. The inside of

the shell is white, with a border of alternating light and dark bars. Outer surface shows about 25 blunt radial ridges. Very common on rocks and pier pilings.

56. FINGERED LIMPET—*Acmaea digitalis* Eschscholtz. Diameter about 1 inch. Apex off-center, slightly hooked forward. Gray, mottled with areas of fine white dots and darker gray lines and streaks. Inside white, with symmetrical brown area at apex. As many as 15 to 25 fairly strong radiating ribs, giving wavy appearance to edge of shell. Extremely common. This shell has often been confused with the mask limpet, *Acmaea persona*, now generally held to be a more northerly species.

57. KELP LIMPET—*Acmaea insessa* (Hinds). Length to ¼ inch. Elliptical, narrow; color light red-brown, surface smooth. May be most easily identified by its habitat, which is usually on the flat center portion of the stipe of the feather-boa kelp, *Egregia*. The limpet eats its way into the kelp, making a depression into which the shell just fits; this pit is not deep enough to come above the apex of the shell. On any piece of *Egregia*, even if you don't find a living limpet, you will find a series of these pits.

58. FILE LIMPET — *Acmaea limatula* Carpenter. Length 1 inch; shell rounded oval, fairly flat, color brown or black. Shell bears radial ribs with a toothed, file-like texture. The muscular foot is black along the sides, white on the bottom. Very common.

59. ROUGH LIMPET—*Acmaea scabra* (Gould). Length to 1¼ inches. Shell oval, with rather low apex placed well forward. Strong radiating ribs (without teeth) with deep grooves between, their ends imparting a deeply scalloped edge to the shell. Very common in the splash zone; one of the high tide level indicators (pl. 6b).

60. OWL LIMPET—*Lottia gigantea* Sowerby. Length to 4 inches—the largest local representative of the true limpets. Outside brown and black in irregular patches,

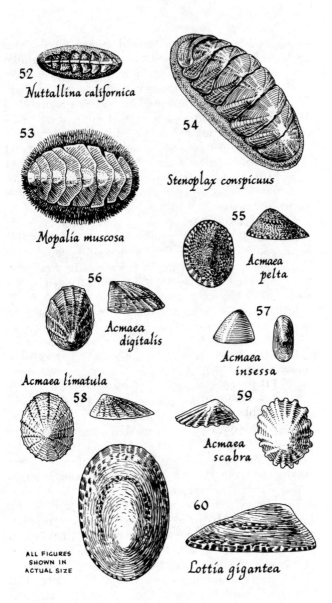

52 *Nuttallina californica*

54

Stenoplax conspicuus

53

Mopalia muscosa

55

Acmaea pelta

56

Acmaea digitalis

57

Acmaea insessa

Acmaea limatula

58

59

Acmaea scabra

ALL FIGURES
SHOWN IN
ACTUAL SIZE

60

Lottia gigantea

usually with cream area toward center. Oval, with low rounded profile. Found fairly high in the middle tide zone, although the larger individuals live lower down. At the apex of the inner surface of the shell, there is a large chestnut marking which remotely resembles the silhouette of a horned owl with its ear-tufts extended straight out (pl. 6c).

The owl limpet spends its daylight hours clamped to its own personal spot on a rock, then wanders about at night to graze on *Ulva* and other nearby seaweeds. Growths of algae are kept clipped short, and resemble well-kept lawns.

THE ABALONES. The coast of California is justly famous for its abalone population; unfortunately, this fame, coupled with the State's increasing population, has decimated the abalones in the intertidal zone, and the visitor is not likely to see any legal-sized specimens unless he can dive to 30 feet.

In its general shape, the abalone resembles a clam shell, and innocent collectors have been known to search vainly for the "other half" of what they take to be a bivalve. It is really a snail, though, and has a single shell, which shows, upon close examination, the spiral structure so typical of the group.

The aperture has become as large as the shelf itself, and is filled, in the living animal, by a tremendous muscular foot. The foot is used by the abalone for locomotion and for clinging tightly to rocks, and by human beings for abalone steaks. The foot is ringed by the fringe of the mantle, which is extended into numerous short sensory tentacles.

There is a row of openings along the top of the shell, and a widespread belief is that their number denotes the age of the abalone. This is not true; each kind of abalone has a restricted range in the number of open holes, and throughout its life the number will be within this range. A close look at an empty shell will show that the holes at the inner end of the line have been closed off, while new holes are added at the outer end; very frequently the outer hole will still be in the process of forming, and will show as a notch on the edge of the shell.

The function of these holes provides an illustration of a basic tenet of the conditions of life: namely, no animal may live long in its own waste products. The holes constitute a primitive but effective method for separating the outgoing and incoming streams of water, allowing waste products to be carried away without polluting the fresh supply. Water passes in under the edge of the shell, goes across the gills, picks up waste, and is discharged through the holes on top of the shell.

The water may be partially used as a conveyor of fine particles of food, but the abalone's chief mode of sustenance is browsing on large seaweeds. The type of food eaten has a direct effect upon the color of the new shell-growth, and a researcher at the Scripps Institution has produced several "rainbow" abalones, with successive growth-areas in strikingly different colors.

The inner surface of the shell is strikingly iridescent, and the abalone has long been valued from an artistic viewpoint as well as from a gastronomic one. The American Indians were great shell traders, and Pacific Coast abalones were carried beyond the Mississippi a thousand years before Columbus.

It is interesting to note that an observant amateur naturalist used the distribution of abalones to prove that Baja California, at that time thought to be a tremendous island, was actually a peninsula. The naturalist was Padre Eusebio Kino. A Jesuit missionary, he was sent to Baja California in 1681, and soon noticed that while abalones were common on the Pacific shores of Baja California, there were none to be found on the Gulf side. When a Mohave Indian admirer presented him with some "blue shells" near what is now

Yuma, Arizona, saying they had been obtained in the ocean straight to the west, Padre Kino realized that the collector must have travelled around the head of the Gulf, and that Baja California must be a peninsula. With characteristic energy he set out to test this notion, and in 1702 reached a point from which he and his ill companion (who died shortly afterward) saw the sun *rise* across the Gulf of California, giving dramatic proof that they had rounded the Gulf and were now on its western shore. Kino thereupon produced a map of the head of the Gulf, and it was to be 200 years before anybody made a better one.

The collecting and possession of abalone in California is strictly governed by laws, and the would-be collector must obtain a fishing license and familiarize himself with all the rules concerning season, size, and bag limits.

Pearls of several shapes and types are not uncommon in abalones and many of these are quite lovely; they have at present, however, no commercial value.

61. BLACK ABALONE — *Haliotis cracherodii* Leach. Length to 8 inches, although 5 is more usual. Five to nine open holes, all flush with the shell (the edges not raised into short tubes). Color black or deep blue on the outside; iridescent white on the inside, with no muscle scar showing. Undersized specimens are fairly common in the lower portions of the intertidal zone.

62. RED ABALONE — *Haliotis rufescens* Swainson. Length to 11 inches—largest of our local abalones. Three or four open holes, with edges raised into low tubular projections. Inside of shell iridescent, with distinctive central muscle scar of concentric lines crossed, in the middle, with a set of much finer parallel "flow" lines. Outside of shell brick red; the red layer projects a little beyond the iridescent inner layer, making a narrow peripheral red band which is visible from the lower side. The top of the shell is usually covered with algae and other marine growths.

Found in surf-swept areas, and to depths of at least 500 feet; living specimens are not often seen in the intertidal zone.

This is perhaps the most popular abalone, from a commercial viewpoint, and is collected by professional divers. It is often available in restaurants.

63. GREEN ABALONE — *Haliotis fulgens* Philippi. Length to 10 inches, average closer to 8. Five to seven open holes, only slightly elevated. Inside of shell highly iridescent with large patches of green and blue, with pink and purple highlights. Muscle scar prominent. Outer surface usually at least partly covered with growth. This species resembles the red abalone, but does not have the red band around the inner margin of the shell. Fairly common in the intertidal zone, although legal-sized specimens are not often found there.

64. GIANT KEYHOLE LIMPET — *Megathura crenulata* (Sowerby). Length of shell to 4 inches; the animal itself is too large to fit completely into the shell, and extends beyond it on all sides. The shell is oval, usually tan or gray, with fine radiating lines of rough texture; there is a single large opening at the apex. The mantle is sometimes black (in which case the pigment will rub off on the hands of a collector), sometimes striped and spotted in grays and browns. It extends beyond the shell, reflexes, and nearly covers the upper surface of the shell. The foot is bright yellow; it may be cut into several steaks, which are edible —but just barely!

65. VOLCANO LIMPET — *Fissurella volcano* Reeve. Length 1 inch. Shell oval, with a single oval opening at the apex. Color usually reddish or purplish, with irregular radiating stripes and streaks of a darker color. Abundant in the middle and lower tide zones.

66. SMOOTH BROWN TURBAN—*Norrisia norrisi* Sowerby. Diameter to 1½ inches. Color rich red-brown. There is a deep umbilicus (a depression at the center

of the whorl on the underside) which is colored bright green. The flesh is bright orange. Most often seen crawling about on the flat stipes and blades of the seaweed *Eisenia*. A species of slipper shell, *Crepidula adunca* (no. 80) is often attached to the shells of smooth brown turbans.

67. BLACK TURBAN SHELL — *Tegula funebralis* (A. Adams). Length to 1½ inches. Shell heavy, deep blue-black; dark covering on parts of the spire is often worn away, revealing the pearly layer beneath. At times, extremely common in the middle tide zone, often found in congregations literally covering the sides of small exposed rocks; even when not seen in such numbers, there are always some individuals about. The empty shells provide homes for many hermit crabs.

68. SPECKLED TURBAN SHELL—*Tegula gallina*(Forbes). Length 1 inch. Shell dark, finely mottled with lighter spots, usually arranged in slanted vertical stripes. Common in the middle tide zone, but not as numerous as the black turban.

69. GILDED TURBAN SHELL — *Tegula aureotincta* (Forbes). Length 1 inch. Color gray-brown. There is a deep umbilicus, the center of which is colored golden orange, often surrounded by a pale blue band. Moderately common in the middle tide zone.

70. WAVY TOP SHELL — *Astraea undosa* (Wood). Length to 4 inches or more. Shell heavy, pearly beneath, covered with a fuzzy brown fibrous covering called a "periostracum." Numerous strong angled vertical ridges on the shell crossed by less distinct parallel spiral ridges. Like many snails, this one has an operculum—a door attached to the soft body parts so arranged as to close up the aperture when the animal withdraws into the shell. The operculum of the wavy top shell is thick and strong, with a smooth brown surface on the inside and strong toothed ribs on the outside. Fairly common in the low tide zones; the

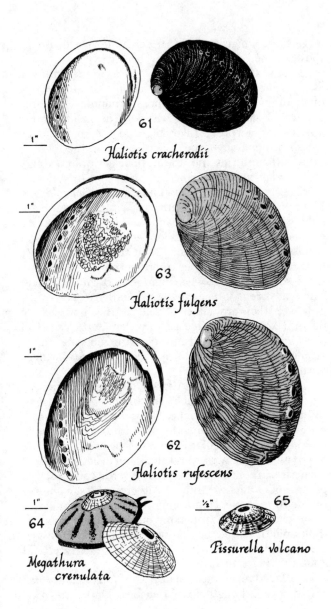

61

Haliotis cracherodii

63

Haliotis fulgens

62

Haliotis rufescens

64

Megathura crenulata

65

Fissurella volcano

largest specimens seen by beach visitors are usually those washed ashore on sandy beaches.

71. CHECKERED PERIWINKLE — *Littorina scutulata* Gould. Shell to ½ inch long, usually smaller. Color often dingy gray, but sometimes a minute checkered pattern of darker spots is visible. The inside of the aperture is purplish. Lives high on the rocks in the splash zone, above the reach of even the highest tides, although this species does not get quite as high as *Littorina planaxis* (no. 72).

72. FLAT-BOTTOMED PERIWINKLE — *Littorina planaxis* Philippi. Length occasionally to ¾ inch. Color variable, sometimes faintly banded. The shape of the columella (the central axis of the shell on the lower surface) is sharply flattened, and this is a diagnostic feature. The periwinkles represent an evolutionary stage somewhere between marine and land animals. They must remain near the sea, in order to keep their gills wet; they are sufficiently terrestrial, however, to down if kept long immersed in water. Both species of periwinkle are abundant in the splash zone, and range all along the Pacific coast of California and northern Mexico.

73. SCALY TUBE SNAIL — *Aletes squamigera* Carpenter. Shell diameter to ½ inch, length to 5 or 6 inches, twisted into irregular shape. Color whitish, with scaly texture. Operculum smooth, purplish-brown. Usually grows in large irregular colonies. This snail starts life as a typical snail with spiral shell, but when it reaches a length of about one millimeter, it settles on a rock or piling and attaches itself. As it grows, it assumes a simple tube shape, conforming to the shape of its substrate, but with the opening of the tube turned at right angles. Its feeding by means of a community net has been described in the section on "The Intertidal Zone as a Place to Live" (p. 27).

74. CALIFORNIA HORN SHELL — *Cerithidea californica* (Haldeman). Length to 1¼ inches. Dark brown or

gray, with distinct vertical ridges. Operculum smooth and brown. Extremely abundant at low tide on exposed mud flats from San Francisco to Mexico. It is a biological axiom that when a species is adapted to living in an environment in which few species are able to live, the successful species may occur in tremendous numbers. That is the case here; the California horn shell is often so abundant as literally to cover the surface of estuarine mud flats (pls. 5a, 6a).

75. COMMON VIOLET SEA SNAIL — *Janthina janthina* (Linnaeus). Diameter to 1 inch. Shell fragile, globe shaped; color violet, deepest at big end of shell, fading almost to white at the small end. This is not an inhabitant of our shore, living rather in the open sea; it is occasionally found after being washed ashore, however. In its home territory, it lives at the surface, keeping itself afloat by means of a self-constructed raft of bubbles, from which it hangs spire-downward. It has often been pointed out that the coloring of the shell is such that the light area, upon which the shell's own shadow falls, is turned away from the light in an application of the universal principle of "countershading," which reduces the animal's visibility. The purple-and-white coloring is typical of the open sea.

76. WHITE WENTLETRAP—*Epitonium tinctum* (Carpenter). Length ½ inch, color white. Each whorl has 12 ridges raised into sharp flat vanes. This animal is found around the bases of large solitary anemones (*Anthopleura xanthogrammica*) upon which it feeds. There are several local species, all quite similar in general appearance.

The word "wentletrap" comes from the Dutch or German, and means a "winding staircase." One Oriental species, the precious wentletrap, was once so diligently sought by wealthy collectors that a clever artist made forgeries of rice flour, and was able to fool several collectors into buying them for high prices. Today, improvement in collecting methods and access to collecting grounds have lowered the monetary worth of the genuine shells, but the forgeries are extremely valuable as works of art!

77. ANCIENT HOOF SHELL—*Hipponix antiquatus* (Linnaeus). Shell ½ to 1 inch in diameter. Shell not spiral, but resembles a gray-white limpet with a wrinkled surface; the apex may be central or near one end. Fairly common in the middle tide zone, often found clinging to other shells.

QUARTER-DECK SHELLS AND THEIR RELATIVES. Members of this superfamily (Calyptraeacea) very much resemble limpets when viewed from above, but the inside of the shell is different in the possession of a sort of shelf or "quarter-deck" which supports certain internal organs. In the cup-and-saucer shells, this shelf is central, and is curved into a sort of cup. There are five families, with many species, on the Pacific Coast.

78. CUP-AND-SAUCER SHELL — *Crucibulum spinosum* (Sowerby). Diameter to 1 inch, shape nearly circular. Outer surface of shell covered with small prickly spines, except for the smooth apex. Interior glossy red-brown, with small white triangular "cup" at one side. Very common in the low tide zone; lives down to at least the 180-foot depth.

79. ONYX SLIPPER SHELL—*Crepidula onyx* Sowerby. Length to 2 inches, color red-brown, occasionally with faint lighter rays. Apex near one end, usually slightly hooked. The interior of the shell varies in color, but the shelf is always white. Fairly common from the middle tide zone down to at least 300 feet, attached to rocks or to other shells.

80. TURBAN SLIPPER SHELL—*Crepidula adunca* Sowerby. Length ½ inch; smooth, brown, with sharply hooked apex near one end. Very common, especially attached to the shell of the smooth brown turban, *Norrisia*. The slipper shells are known as "protandrous hermaphrodites" because they all start life as males,

66

Norrisia norrisii

67

Tegula
funebralis

68

Tegula
gallina

Astraea undosa

70

69

Tegula aureotincta

71

Littorina
scutulata

72

Littorina
planaxis

74

Cerithidea
californica

75

Janthina janthina

76

Epitonium tinctum

73

Aletes
squamigerus

77

Hipponix antiquatus

78

Crucibulum spinosum

79

Crepidula onyx

80

Crepidula adunca

ALL SHOWN AT
APPROXIMATELY
NATURAL SIZE.

then change to females as they grow older.

81. DOVE SHELL—*Erato columbella* Menke. Length ¼ inch. Short spire, aperture long with minute teeth along the whitish edges. General color red-brown or gray, surface smooth. Occasionally seen in the middle tide zone. Although human collectors do not often come across live shells, the sea gulls apparently know better where to find them; gull droppings are often seen to contain large numbers of dove shells.

There are many other species of tiny shells on our coasts, and one of the best ways to find them is to sift coarse beach sand through a tea strainer. The dove shell is presented as just one example of this almost microfauna.

82. LITTLE COFFEE-BEAN—*Trivia californiana* (Gray). Length to ½ inch. Shell has 10 to 12 cross ridges which are interrupted at the midline by a pale, shallow groove. Color gray or pinkish, ribs lighter. Fairly common in the low tide zone, especially among the seaweed *Eisenia.*

83. LARGE COFFEE-BEAN—*Trivia solandri* (Sowerby). Length to ¾ inch. Ribs interrupted by a deeper groove than in the preceding species; at the point of interruption, the ribs have large knobs. Fairly common from San Pedro southward; often found together with no. 82.

84. CHESTNUT COWRY — *Cypraea (Zonaria) spadicea* Swainson. Length to 2 inches. Color white beneath, fading to purplish brown on the sides and rich chestnut brown on top, usually with darker spots and blotches. Mantle, when extruded, is sandy, with flecks of brown and black. Shell nearly round in cross section. Fairly common in the low tide zone from Monterey south; abundant among rocks in the bottom of the kelp beds at depths of 30 to 80 feet.

There has been much confusion as to the proper name of this species and its many relatives, with authorities proposing scores of new names. I have followed the lead of Dr. Myra Keen, perhaps the leading malacologist of the Pacific Coast, in retaining the old genus *Cypraea*, and using *Zonaria* as a sub-genus.

The cowries constitute a group of snails with shells whose bright colors and glossy surfaces have made them attractive to humans since the earliest times. In many civilizations they have been used for money, a use which gave us the Chinese word "cash" (oddly enough, unrelated to the English word "cash"). The Chinese cash is a perforated coin which was handled by being strung on cords. This method of stringing is said to have originated where cowry shells were used as the medium of exchange, and the word itself is an onomatopoetic representation of the sound made when a string of cowry shells is shaken to signify a readiness to bargain.

Infant cowries show the typical spiral snail shape, but change as they approach maturity. The outer lip of the aperture turns inward, and the shell becomes almost symmetrical along the line of the narrow slit-like aperture. The spire is obliterated by a layer of glossy enamel. This enamel, which covers the entire exterior of the shell, is secreted by glands in the edge of the mantle. When a cowry is undisturbed, the mantle is extended and reflexed so as to cover the entire shell; upon any disturbance, the mantle slides around and disappears into the aperture. The deposition of new shell material from the outside, coupled with the polishing action of the sliding mantle, imparts to cowries their high gloss.

The majority of the cowries, of which there are hundreds of species, live in tropical waters, but there are several along the California coast, of which three are considered here. Please note that the first two (preceding nos. 82 and 83) do *not* have the glossy shells so typical of the group.

85. RECLUZ'S MOON SHELL — *Polinices reclusianus*

(Deshayes). Diameter to 2½ inches, globular; a large, heavy shell. Exterior smooth, light brown or gray, often with cloudy reddish blotches; operculum red-brown, translucent. There is a large shell callus almost or completely covering the umbilicus. Fairly common in the lower part of the middle tide zone, especially in connection with sandy bottoms.

86. LEWIS'S MOON SHELL—*Lunatia lewisi* (Gould). Diameter to 5 inches, globular, fairly heavy. Umbilicus deep and narrow, *not* usually covered by a shell callus as in the preceding species, which it otherwise resembles rather closely.

Both moon shells are carnivorous, preying mostly on clams, which they kill and eat by drilling through the clams' shells with their file-like radulae. The moon shells have a foot that is much bigger than the shell, seemingly impossible to retract all the way; the foot contains a great deal of water, however, and when this is slowly expelled, the entire foot can be drawn back and the operculum closed. The moon shells are found predominantly in bays and other quiet waters. They lay their eggs in rubbery "collars" consisting of sand grains and thousands of eggs cemented together; these egg cases are common on the sand and mud of quiet bays, especially in the summer months.

87. THREE-CORNERED TROPHON — *Trophonopsis triangulata* (Carpenter). Length 1 inch. Color gray, with white aperture. Found all along the Southern California coast, but never very common.

This is one of the rock shells, of the family Muricidae, the murex group. Most of the rock shells are tropical, and they number in their ranks some of the most beautiful sorts of shells; some collectors make a specialty of them. As so often happens in interesting families, this one has received quite a bit of taxonomic attention resulting in name-changing of a rather bewildering sort. The three-cornered trophon will be found in many shell books as *Boreotrophon; Tropho-*

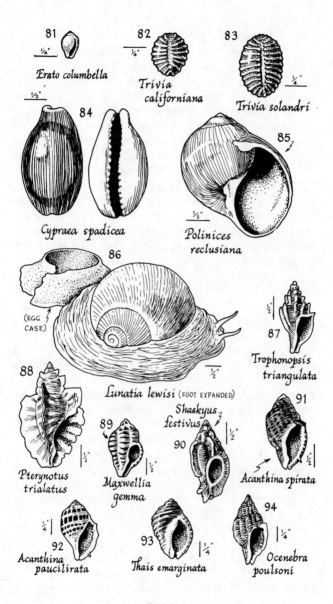

81 Erato columbella ¼"

82 Trivia californiana ¼"

83 Trivia solandri ¼"

84 Cypraea spadicea ½"

85 Polinices reclusiana ½"

86 (EGG CASE) Lunatia lewisi (FOOT EXPANDED) ½"

87 Trophonopsis triangulata ½"

88 Pterynotus trialatus ½"

89 Maxwellia gemma ½"

90 Shaskyus festivus ½"

91 Acanthina spirata ½"

92 Acanthina paucilirata ¼"

93 Thais emarginata ¼"

94 Ocenebra poulsoni ¼"

nopsis, however, is preferable.

88. THREE-WINGED MUREX — *Pterynotus trialatus* (Sowerby). Length 2 to 3 inches. Three wide vertical vanes extend radially from the shell, with smooth spaces between them. Color light brown, sometimes with fine white spiral bands. Not common; generally found alive only well offshore. Some books will list *Pterynotus carpenteri* and *Pterynotus petri,* but many malacologists believe these to be only subspecies, or even ecological varieties, of *P. trialatus.*

89. GEM MUREX — *Maxwellia gemma* (Sowerby). Length 1 inch. A short and chunky shell, with six rounded vertical ridges with sharp valleys between. Spire with several deep, irregular pits. Color white with brown or gray cross stripes. Aperture small. Not uncommon in the extreme low tide zone, and may be found higher up, especially in association with the scaly tube snail, *Aletes.*

90. FESTIVE MUREX — *Shaskyus festivus* (Hinds). Length to 1½ inches. Spire high; canal closed over to form a tube from the aperture to the tip. Frilled vertical ridges, recurved at their outer edges, with rounded ridges between. Color pale brown, with fine spiral lines of darker brown. Fairly common south of Santa Barbara, in both rocky and muddy areas; also found on pier pilings, under overhanging seaweeds.

91. ANGULAR UNICORN SHELL — *Acanthina spirata* (Blainville). Length to 1½ inches. A sharp angle occurs at the shoulder, so that the spire is turreted. Color gray or brown, often with a greenish tinge, with numerous fine broken dark lines, running spirally. Aperture blue-white, with a prominent spine near the lower end of the outer lip. Canal open. Common in rocky areas at middle tide; at times (especially in winter) extremely abundant.

92. CHECKERED UNICORN SHELL—*Acanthina paucilirata* (Stearns). Length to 1 inch, but usually smaller. Fatter than the preceding species, and with a lower

spire. Color white or gray with regular rows of square dark markings. Smooth inner part of lip usually tinged a deep purple. Very common south of Los Angeles, although never quite so abundant as the angular unicorn shell.

93. ROCK THAIS — *Thais emarginata* (Deshayes). Diameter to 1 inch. Usually globose in shape, although some individuals are rather long and narrow. Aperture round, large, with thin outer lip; interior red-brown or purple. Shell sculptured with strong spiral ridges, often large and small in alternation. Abundant.

94. POULSON'S DWARF TRITON — *Ocenebra poulsoni* (Carpenter). Length 1 to 2 inches. Shell heavy, spire fairly high; about nine vertical, knobby ridges crossed by spiral lines of various sizes, although living specimens may be covered with a thin brown periostracum hiding this pattern. Three or four small teeth on outer edge of aperture; interior white. Very common from middle tide zone down, found among rocks and on pier pilings.

95. NUTTALL'S HORNMOUTH—*Pterorytis nuttalli* (Conrad). Length to 2 inches. Gray or yellowish with red-brown markings. Canal may be open in young specimens, but is closed in adults. Most larger individuals have a "horn" or tooth near the base of the outer lip. Fairly common in the low tide zone south of Santa Barbara. The systematic position of this shell is uncertain, and it will be found listed as *Ceratostoma* and *Purpura* as well as *Pterorytis*.

96. KELLET'S WHELK — *Kelletia kelleti* (Forbes). Length to 6 inches. Usually beige or straw-colored, often overgrown with algae, bryozoans, or other organisms. Shell heavy; aperture white and glossy. Surface marked with very fine spiral grooves crossing vertical rounded ridges. This shell grows slowly and lives long: MacGinitie says that a 3-inch individual is probably 7 or 8 years old. *Kelletia* is common at depths of 30 feet or more, often being encountered

by scuba divers at the bottom of the kelp bed. Dead shells are washed ashore fairly often.

97. LIVID MACRON — *Macron lividus* A. Adams. Length occasionally to 1 inch. Pale brown shell covered with thick, dark brown, cloth-like periostracum, often worn away in spots. Aperture white, columella polished. Very common under rocks in the low tide zone from Santa Barbara to central Baja California.

98. CHANNELED DOG WHELK — *Nassarius fossatus* (Gould). Length occasionally to 2 inches. Color yellow-gray to orange-brown; columella covered with a glossy callus of bright orange in mature individuals. Outer lip with jagged edge. Common all along the California coast, most abundant in mud flats. Like all the dog whelks (which are also called basket shells), this species is a scavenger, and locates its food by smell.

99. PURPLE OLIVE SHELL—*Olivella biplicata* (Sowerby). Length to 1 inch. Color usually blue-purple or blue-gray, although a few are almost white. Surface glossy. Columella with white callus showing two folds. Abundant in sandy and rock areas of the low tide zone, especially in the summer; one of our most abundant seashells. The purple olive often crawls through the sand just under the surface, leaving a mole-like furrow of displaced sand behind it. This is a popular shell among small hermit crabs who are seeking a home.

100. IDA'S MITRE SHELL—*Mitra idae* Melvill. Length to 2¼ inches. Shell brown, but in fresh, unworn specimens, is covered with a jet black periostracum which is marked with fine spiral threads. The narrow aperture is white. Occasionally found under rocks at the lowest tide level. This is a handsome shell, although its somber coloring is in marked contrast to the bright orange of some of the tropical mitre shells.

101. CALIFORNIA CONE SHELL — *Conus californicus* Reeve. Length to 1 inch. Shell yellow-brown, often

with a single blue-gray spiral band; in life, covered with a velvety dark brown or bluish periostracum. This is quite a drab shell compared to some of its tropical relatives; the cone shells in general are quite decorative. All of them are carnivorous, and have a beautifully designed mechanism for planting poisoned darts in their prey or their attackers. Some species are extremely dangerous to handle, having been known to bring death to humans; the California cone, however, has never been implicated in a human sting.

102. GOULD'S BUBBLE SHELL—*Bulla gouldiana* Pilsbry. Length to 2 inches. Shell globose, fragile. Color pinkish gray, with cloudy dark markings bordered on their left edges with white. Very common in the quiet waters of our fast-vanishing lagoons and estuaries. The body of this tectibranch snail is too large to be completely withdrawn into the shell, and when it is active, its shell is entirely enveloped by the reflexed mantle.

This and the following species lay yellow strings of eggs whose tangled skeins are a familiar sight along bay shores.

103. WHITE BUBBLE SHELL — *Haminoea vesicula* (Gould). Length to 1 inch. Color white or yellowbrown; shell extremely fragile. Quite similar in looks and habits to no. 102, but lighter colored and usually only half as long.

104. BAY SEA HARE — *Navanax inermis* (Cooper). Length to 6 inches. No shell. Body elongate, usually black with many bright yellow dots and dashes, and vivid blue lines, especially along the edges of the body. Belongs to the same big group (tectibranchs) as the bubble shells, but lacks the shell. The bay sea hare is abundant in estuarine waters, and is occasionally found in rocky tide pools on the outer coast. It is carnivorous, and seems to prefer white bubble shells to any other food; these it swallows whole, and picking up a feeding specimen is like picking up a

[93]

bag of marbles. The eggs are laid in tangled masses of yellow strings, and may be found throughout the year.

105. SEA HARE — *Aplysia californica* (Cooper). Length to 1 foot. The mottled brown or purplish sea hare is a common sight in the middle tide zone and lower, particularly in rocky areas; the larger individuals are seen only at low tide. The sea hare is a vegetarian, browsing on various sorts of seaweed, including kelp, and has a complicated multi- "stomached" digestive system which is able to cope with such food. When disturbed, the sea hare emits a deep purple ink, for which it is sometimes called the inkfish—a name held in common with the squid and several other creatures.

These animals are hermaphroditic, and each individual possesses a full set of both male and female reproductive organs. They cannot fertilize their own eggs, however, but must copulate with another individual, operating either as male or female or, where several individuals are involved, as both at once. The eggs are laid in long yellow strings which are formed into masses as big as grapefruit. The number of eggs contained in one of these masses is staggering; Mac-Ginitie has estimated that a large sea hare may lay as many as half a billion eggs every year! The larvae hatch out in 10 or 12 days, and during their free-swimming period, the vast majority of them fall prey to the various plankton eaters. One shudders to think what would happen if this slaughter did not occur; the young would grow to full size and produce billions of eggs in their turn, and in a few years the combined mass of sea hares would be greater than the whole earth—a prospect of doom compared to which either fire or ice sounds almost pleasant.

106. BLACK SEA HARE — *Aplysia vaccaria* Winkler. Similar in shape to the preceding species, but has a black rough skin instead of a slick brown one, and it

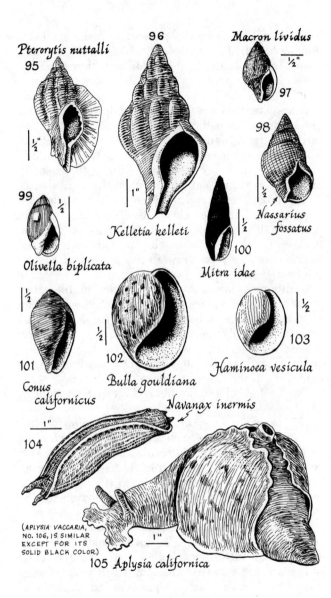

Pterorytis nuttalli
95

96

Macron lividus
½"
97

98

½
Nassarius fossatus

99
½

Olivella biplicata

Kelletia kelleti

1"

½
100

Mitra idae

½
101

½
102

½
103

Haminoea vesicula

Conus californicus

Bulla gouldiana

Navanax inermis

1"
104

(APLYSIA VACCARIA, NO. 106, IS SIMILAR EXCEPT FOR ITS SOLID BLACK COLOR.)

1"

105 *Aplysia californica*

[95]

is much the larger of the two; some black sea hares attain a length of 30 inches and a weight of 35 pounds. Found mainly in the kelp beds offshore, but occasionally in low tide pools.

THE NUDIBRANCHS constitute a group of snails without shells, many members of which are brightly colored. The term "nudibranch" (pronounced NUDE-ee-brank) means "exposed gills"; the gills (technically known as "cerata") are exposed, without the covering of a shell or even a flap of skin as in the tectibranchs. In one group, the aeolid nudibranchs, these gills form a fringe all along the sides of the body, form several pairs of gill groups, or are spread evenly all over the back; in the dorid nudibranchs, the gills are gathered together in a tree-like cluster on the posterior part of the back.

Nudibranchs are most often found in the still waters of tide pools, often concealed beneath the lip of an overhanging edge. All are apparently carnivorous, and some have highly specialized diets; a few types limit themselves to sponges, while others eat only hydroids. In some of them, the digestive tract has long fingers extending to the tips of the cerata.

Only a few of our nudibranchs can be presented here.

107. LEMON NUDIBRANCH—*Anisodoris nobilis* (MacFarland). Length to 4 inches. Color orange-yellow or lemon-yellow, with a sprinkling of black dots; skin coarsely granular. This is the largest of our nudibranchs, and is seen occasionally in the tide pools; it is most abundant, however, near the bottoms of the pilings at the outer ends of long piers.

108. RED SPONGE NUDIBRANCHS — *Rostanga pulchra* MacFarland. Length to ¾ inch. Color solid red. Usually found living on (both as substrate and food) red encrusting sponges. The long flat ribbons of eggs are also red. This animal provides an example of

PLATE 1

a) HIGH TIDE early on a fall morning.

b) LOW TIDE about eight hours later on the same day.

c) SURF. Even on a quiet day, intertidal animals must be able to resist or escape the crashing surf.

PLATE 2

a) SPLASH ZONE. Above the reach of the highest tides, this zone is wetted only by the splash and spray from high waves.

b) HIGH TIDE ZONE. Nearly every high tide reaches these rocks. The green covering is a green alga, *Enteromorpha*, the sea felt.

c) MIDDLE TIDE ZONE. The zone of the mussel beds, this area is wet as often as it is dry.

PLATE 3

a) A SEAWEED HABITAT. The thick fronds of the rockweed, *Pelvetia*, provide a protected home for thousands of small creatures.

b) TIDE POOL. The receding tide leaves small bodies of water trapped among the rocks.

c) LOW TIDE ZONE. Animals in this zone are exposed to the air only during the lower tides. Here a red sponge, *Plocamia karykina* (no. 6), may be seen behind the stipes of the southern palm kelp *Eisenia*.

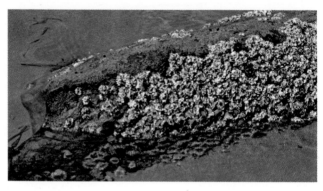

PLATE 4

a) AGGREGATE ANEMONE, *Anthopleura elegantissima* (no. 28). The massed anemones on the face of the rock are almost covered with bits of shell and other debris.

b) AGGREGATE ANEMONE. When covered by water, the individual anemones unfold into the familiar flower shape.

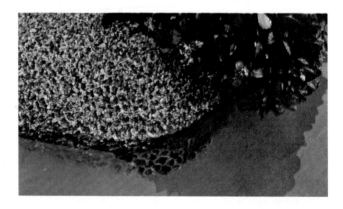

c) SOLITARY GREEN ANEMONE, *Anthopleura xanthogrammica* (no. 27). This species lives at a lower level, and is not so often exposed to the air.

PLATE 5

a) MUD FLAT. The exposed mud-bar is thickly sprinkled with living California horn shells, *Cerithidea californica* (no. 74).

b) CALIFORNIA HORNSHELL, *Cerithidea californica* (no. 74). Each shell is half an inch long. Where they occur at all, they occur by the thousand.

c) SAND-CASTLE WORM, *Phragmatopoma californica* (no. 48). This 15-inch colony is constructed of sand grains cemented together with mucus.

PLATE 6

a) MOSSY CHITON, *Mopalia muscosa*
(no. 53). A small one-inch specimen.

b) ROUGH LIMPET, *Acmaea scabra* (no.
59). Also shown are the WHITE BUCK-
SHOT BARNACLE *Balanus glandula* (no.
155) and the BROWN BUCKSHOT BAR-
NACLE, *Chthamalus fissus* (no. 156).

c) OWL LIMPET, *Lottia gigantea* (no.
60), with the reddish THATCHED BAR-
NACLE *Tetraclita squamosa* (no. 157).

PLATE 7

a) CALIFORNIA MUSSEL, *Mytilus californianus* (no. 114). This is the typical shape of a mussel colony attached to a pier piling, shown at low tide.

b) A closer view of California mussels, together with an OCHRE STARFISH *Pisaster ochraceus* (no. 204), which preys upon them.

PLATE 8

a) OCHRE STARFISH *Pisaster ochraceus* (no. 204) comes in a wide variety of colors.

b) GOOSE BARNACLES *Pollicipes polymerus* (no. 158). These barnacles, the ochre starfish, and the California mussel have been called the Big Three of the surf-swept outer rocky coast of California.

c) WHITE BUCKSHOT BARNACLES *Balanus glandula* (no. 155) and BROWN BUCKSHOT BARNACLES *Chthamalus fissus* (no. 156) are extremely abundant in the high tide and splash zones.

concealing coloration, as it is just the color of its sponge habitat. The concealing effect is lessened, however, by the nudibranch's habit of eating the sponge right down to the bare rock as it crawls along, leaving a distinct rock-colored line pointing directly to the nudibranch's position.

109. BLUE AND GOLD NUDIBRANCH—*Glossodoris californiensis* (Bergh). Length to 1½ inches. Color deep royal blue, with brilliant golden-orange stripes and spots. The specific name, *californiensis*, is said to have been bestowed in honor of the University of California, whose colors are blue and gold. Moderately common at lowest tides.

110. ORCHID NUDIBRANCH — *Glossodoris macfarlandi* Cockerell. Length to ½ inch. Ground color rich orchid purple, with markings of bright orange. Fairly common at low tide.

111. ROSE NUDIBRANCH—*Hopkinsia rosacea* MacFarland. Length to 1 inch. Body a uniform rose color, covered with long flexible processes; these are not gills, however; this animal is of the dorid group, and its gill cluster, almost hidden by the filaments, is at the posterior end. Named by MacFarland for the Hopkins Marine Station, the Pacific Grove facility maintained by Stanford University.

112. PURPLE FAN NUDIBRANCH — *Flabellina iodinea* (Cooper). Length 1½ inches. Body compressed (higher than wide), of a bright purple color, with fringing cerata of bright orange. Abundant at unpredictable times in the middle and lower tide zones. Like several other nudibranchs, this one often crawls along, upside down, hanging from the surface film of the water in a tide pool. If dislodged from its contact with the surface, it sinks toward the bottom; while sinking, it usually makes violent thrashing motions, curving its whole body first to one side and then the other in a manner that causes it to "swim" in an erratic manner.

113. HERMISSENDA—*Hermissenda crassicornis* (Esch-

scholtz). Length to 1 inch. Body usually white or pearly gray, with prominent central longitudinal lines of iridescent blue. The cerata form a fringe along the sides, although close examination shows them to be gathered in several pairs of clusters. Color of cerata variable—may be brown, red, or blue, often tipped with yellow. Abundant at times in the low tide area. This is one of the species known to eat hydroids. Hydroids are generally protected by their stinging nematocysts, but these do not deter this nudibranch; in fact, some are ingested, still in the undischarged state, and pass into the outer tips of the cerata, where they furnish protection to their new host!

Class PELECYPODA (The clams and mussels)

The term "Pelecypoda" means "hatchet-foot," and the muscular foot in some species may indeed remotely resemble a hatchet. Even so, it is not really a very good descriptive term, but I prefer it to the "bivalvia" that has come into recent use. One reason is that most of the other molluscs are named for some feature of their feet, and there is a nice euphony to "Gastropod, Pelecypod, Scaphopod, Cephalopod," etc. Another is that "bivalvia" means "two shells," and while it is generally appropriate, it is now known that some snails (such as *Berthelina*) also have two valves, so the term loses its distinctiveness.

In any event, the characteristic members of this class have two shells, or valves—a right one and a left one—which most often fit quite closely together. They are opened and closed by large muscles connecting the two.

114. CALIFORNIA MUSSEL—*Mytilus californianus* Conrad. Length to 9 inches, but specimens of more than 5 inches are not common in the intertidal zone. Periostracum brown, usually worn away near the beaks to expose the blue-gray shell beneath. Shell with strong ribs, especially around the unworn outer edges.

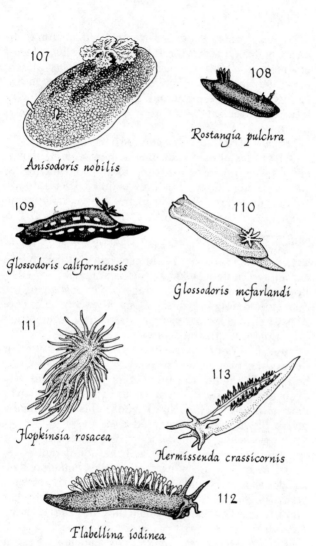

107

Anisodoris nobilis

108

Rostangia pulchra

109

Glossodoris californiensis

110

Glossodoris mcfarlandi

111

Hopkinsia rosacea

113

Hermissenda crassicornis

112

Flabellina iodinea

The California mussel is extremely common on rocky outer shores all along the Pacific Coast, living in great colonies attached to rocks or pilings. This attachment, which is an effective one, is made by means of byssus threads—numerous horny filaments with the free end attached to the rock and the other end to the mussel.

Mussels attach not only to the rocks, but to already-attached mussels, thus forming a thick series of layers among which many other kinds of animals find shelter and food. Prof. MacGinitie once counted 625 California mussels in an area about 10 inches square, and among them he collected 4086 other creatures of 22 different kinds.

The orange flesh of this mussel makes fine fish bait, and is also excellent as human food, although not considered quite as good as the bay mussel (no. 115). Both species may contain dangerous quantities of the mussel-poisoning organism *Gonyaulax catenella* (no. 2) and should be eaten only after due consideration of season and quarantine rules.

Mussel beds are associated with the upper part of the middle tide zone. An interesting feature of these beds is that while the number of mussels gradually decreases toward the upper limit of the bed, the lower limit is marked by a sharp cutoff; this is especially noticeable in the more exposed areas.

The goose barnacle *Pollicipes* is sometimes almost as numerous as the mussel, and the population is referred to by ecologists as the "*Mytilus-Pollicipes*" association. Also abundant among them is the starfish *Pisaster ochraceus*, making the third member of what Ricketts and Calvin have called "the Big Three of the wave-swept outer coast" (pls. 2c, 7a, 7b).

115. BAY MUSSEL—*Mytilus edulis* Linnaeus. Length to 4 inches. Color brown-black; shell smooth, without the radiating ribs of the preceding species. Sometimes found on rocky outer coasts, but intertidally more

common in bays; below the intertidal zone, it may be found in great bunches on the lines of moorings and marker buoys. This is the most highly prized mussel from the gastronomic viewpoint, and is the same species served as "moules" in better restaurants in France; rather surprisingly, however, it is not eaten in great numbers in California.

116. GREAT HORSE MUSSEL—*Modiolus modiolus* Linnaeus. Length to 9 inches. Similar to California mussel, but the shell showing through the thick periostracum is usually chalk white. Also, as in all the horse mussels, the shell extends beyond the beaks, while in the California and bay mussels, the beaks are at the very end. The periostracum of the horse mussel forms a rough "beard" near the edges of the shell. This species does not of itself form beds or clusters, although it is often associated with beds of the other two species; it may be completely solitary, especially when living in quiet waters of sandy estuaries.

117. BRANCH - RIBBED MUSSEL — *Septifer bifurcatus* (Conrad). Length to 2 inches, shape almost triangular. Prominent radiating ribs, some of which branch. The inside of the shell shows a little "deck" near the small end. Fairly common in the intertidal zone, occurring singly rather than in beds.

118. DATE MUSSEL—*Lithophaga plumula* (Hanley). Length to 2 inches; shape very much like a date seed. The name *"Lithophaga"* means rock-eating, and is most appropriate in a metaphorical way, for this mussel drives its round tunnels into rocks, clay, and into other shells. It does not actually eat the rock, of course, but in typical bivalve fashion lives upon minute particles strained by its gills from the water.

119. NATIVE OYSTER—*Ostrea lurida* Carpenter. Diameter to 2½ inches. Shells thin, fairly flat, rounded but irregular; usually shows coarse concentric growth lines. Color (outside) varies from gray-white to purple-black, sometimes with bands of purple or maroon.

Interior moderately shiny, ranging from gray to olive green, often with metallic sheen. Found in sheltered waters, attached to practically any kind of solid object. Abundant. This is the same species that is sold in the Pacific Northwest as the Olympia oyster, and is most delectable.

120. SPECKLED SCALLOP — *Aequipecten circularis* (Sowerby). Diameter to 3½ inches. Color variable, usually some shade of light brown with darker (often purplish) markings. Ribs rounded. The speckled scallop was formerly abundant in bays, but has been depleted, by direct human predation and by the loss of its estuarine habitat, to the point where legal control became necessary. Before you take any specimens, be sure to check California Fish and Game regulations; at the present time, there is *no* open season.

The scallops are among the most alert and "intelligent" of the pelecypods, in that some of their reactions are rapid, and therefore readily understandable in human terms. They have the most complex nervous system in their class, and many species possess quite highly developed eyes, appearing as little bright buttons between the tentacles fringing the mantle. Scallops are quite active as swimmers, their swimming being a method of escape from enemies such as certain kinds of starfishes. In swimming, the shells are rapidly clapped together, like a pair of self-powered castanets. With each closing of the shells, water is forced out between them through valves at the hinge, producing a jet of water which propels the animal forward. The motion is toward the open side of the shells, with the hinge as the trailing edge.

Scallops are among the finest of sea foods.

121. SAN DIEGO SCALLOP—*Pecten diegensis* Dall. Diameter to 5 inches. Ribs are flat-topped. The right shell is deeply arched, while the left one is almost flat, and is usually darker in color than the right. This is a lovely shell, not often found in the intertidal area.

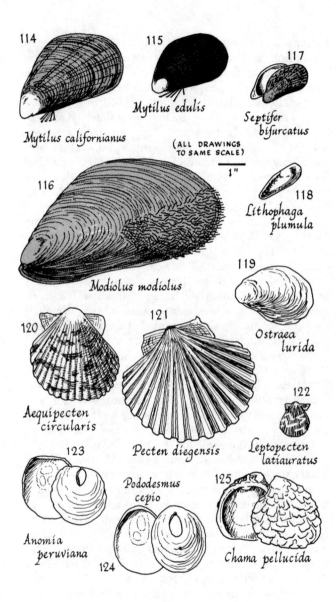

114
Mytilus californianus

115
Mytilus edulis

117
Septifer bifurcatus

(ALL DRAWINGS TO SAME SCALE)

1"

116
Modiolus modiolus

118
Lithophaga plumula

119
Ostraea lurida

120
Aequipecten circularis

121
Pecten diegensis

122
Leptopecten latiauratus

123
Anomia peruviana

Pododesmus cepio

124

125
Chama pellucida

Indians have long favored this shell as a base for decoration, and the Navajos of Arizona are still using them; some of their most beautiful pieces are entire shells, inlaid with turquoise and other materials.

122. KELP SCALLOP — *Leptopecten latiauratus* (Conrad). Diameter about 1 inch. Valves fairly flat, very thin and fragile; color yellow or brown or orange, usually with zigzag white cross stripes. Population subject to tremendous variation; years may go by without the presence of very many of these scallops, then one year there will be untold millions of them, attached to seaweed—especially the elk kelp, *Pelagophycus*.

123. PEARLY JINGLE SHELL — *Anomia peruviana* d'Orbigny. Diameter to 2 inches; shape very irregular. The shell is thin, translucent and pearly, often with a greenish cast. Takes on the contours of its substrate. Attached by byssus threads, which pass through a deep notch in the right shell, which is always lowermost. The inner surface of the left shell shows three muscle scars. Dead shells extremely abundant, living specimens less often seen.

124. ABALONE JINGLE SHELL — *Pododesmus cepio* (Gray). Diameter rarely to 4 inches; 1 inch more usual. Exterior gray-white, interior white to green. Coarse irregular radiating ribs. Large notch in lower shell, only two muscle scars in upper (left) one. Very abundant in our area, attached to rocks, pier pilings, and especially the shells of the red abalone.

125. AGATE CHAMA—*Chama pellucida* Sowerby. Diameter to 3 inches. Color white, sometimes (especially in young specimens) with red tinge. The young specimens have square-tipped frills set in concentric rows; these frills are translucent (the word *"pellucida"* means "clear.") Abundant on outer coast, attached to any sort of solid substrate, or to floating objects. The two valves are of unequal size, but fit together like a cunningly contrived jewel box. Attachment is by the left valve, with the right one acting as the lid.

[104]

126. REVERSED CHAMA—*Pseudochama exogyra* (Conrad). Similar in size, shape, and color to the agate chama, but attached to the substrate by the right valve. When viewed from the inside, this valve turns to the left, counterclockwise. The two species are often found together.

127. LITTLE HEART SHELL—*Glans carpenteri* Lamy. Length ½ inch. Color brown outside, usually green or purple within. The heavy ribs and squarish outline will serve to distinguish this shell from any other of our region. It has been listed under several names, including *Glans minuscula* and *Cardita subquadrata*.

128. STOUT HEART SHELL—*Cardita ventricosa* Gould. Length 1 inch. Shape circular, with prominent beaks, color dead-white; live specimens have a velvety brown periostracum. About 13 radial ribs. In Southern California, this species lives offshore, but the shells are abundant on beaches built up with dredged-up sand.

129. COMMON EGGSHELL COCKLE—*Laevicardium substriatum* Conrad. Diameter 1 inch. Color light brown, usually with fine interrupted radial markings. Interior of shell yellow, with purple blotches. Outer surface smooth, with faint pattern of radiating ribs. Abundant in bays and estuaries.

130. PISMO CLAM—*Tivela stultorum* (Mawe). Length to over 7 inches. Valves thick, with varnished appearance. The ligament is prominent, looking like brown horn. Color variable, but always some shade of light brown; many individuals are marked with radial dark brown lines fanning out from the umbones. Lives in flat sandy beaches, where it buries itself down to 6 inches or so.

The pismo clam is one of the noblest of seafoods, and in some areas has been hunted almost to the vanishing point. There are now strict laws governing its capture and possession.

The clam takes its name from the area of Pismo Beach, rather than the other way around; "pismo" is an Indian word for "tar," and no one is quite certain how this applies to the Beach.

While preparing pismo clams for the table, some people are surprised to find in its flesh a pencil-shaped object that looks like clear plastic, and are suspicious of it as an unnatural foreign object. It is quite natural, however, being common to many pelecypods and gastropods; it is the "crystalline style," which contains a storehouse of the enzyme amylase, without which the animal cannot digest starch. The style is largest when the clam has been fasting.

131. WHITE VENUS — *Amiantis callosa* (Conrad). Length to 4 inches. Color white. Heavy shell marked with concentric round ridges; no radiating ribs. Rarely lives in the intertidal zone, but shells are rather often washed ashore.

132. WAVY CHIONE—*Chione undatella* (Sowerby). Diameter to 2½ inches. Fairly prominent radial ribs, although these are somewhat obscured by the closely spaced, continuous concentric ridges crossing them. Color gray or white, sometimes with purplish blotches. Dead shells usually bleached dead white; abundant, especially on filled beaches.

133. SMOOTH CHIONE—*Chione fluctifraga* (Sowerby). Diameter to 3½ inches. Rather similar to no. 132, but its radial ribs are more prominent than its concentric ridges, and the ridges are not raised into vanes. Live specimens yellowish. Common in mud flats south of Los Angeles.

134. COMMON LITTLENECK — *Protothaca staminea* (Conrad). Length to 2 inches. Very fine radial ribs crossed by slightly less prominent concentric, rounded ridges, the crossing of the two sets of lines imparting a beaded appearance. Color variable; in sheltered waters, it is most often a uniform gray or brown, while those living on the open coast are usually lighter, with geometric dark brown markings. Edible, and much sought after. Abundant.

135. BENT-NOSE CLAM — *Macoma nasuta* (Conrad). Length to 2 inches. Shell fragile, white, partly covered with thin gray periostracum. Posterior end elongated and bent to the right. This clam habitually buries itself in the mud, lying on its side with the bent tip pointing upward. The siphons protrude from the tip, the incurrent siphon reaching above the surface of the sandy bottoms under quiet waters; it bends down until its tip just touches the surface. Water flowing into this siphon causes it to act like a vacuum cleaner in pulling detritus from the sand. When the clam has cleaned all of the surface it can reach, it moves to a new location. Common.

136. WHITE SAND CLAM—*Macoma secta* (Conrad). Length to 4½ inches. Rather similar to the bent-nose clam, but larger, and without the bent tip. Less common, but not rare in muddy estuaries.

137. YELLOW APOLYMETIS — *Apolymetis biangulata* (Carpenter). Length to 3 inches. Valves asymmetrical, oval. Yellow-brown, covered with irregular thin gray periostracum. Interior of shell glossy white, suffused near the center with clear yellow or peach; this color fades soon after the death of the animal. Fairly common in coarse sand and gravel in quiet waters, and buried in sand among rocks on the outer beaches.

138. BEAN CLAM—*Donax gouldi* Dall. Length to a little over 1 inch. Shells strong. Color extremely variable, ranging from white to chocolate brown or deep blue-gray, often yellow, orange, or purplish. Many individuals show a pattern of darker or lighter bands, either radial or concentric. Dead shells, before the two valves become completely separated, usually gape widely, and in this position are sometimes called "sea butterflies."

The numbers of this clam are as variable as its color. In some years, portions of the beach are covered with a solid pavement of bean clams, lying several layers thick; in other years, there is not a one to be

[107]

seen. The late Prof. Wesley Coe of the Scripps Institution of Oceanography once made a public offer of one dollar for the first live bean clam found on the beach, and several years went by before the reward was claimed. The years of abundance do not appear to form any kind of predictable cycle or pattern. There were especially memorable resurgences of the population in 1910, 1915 (that was the year canneries were set up to prepare bean clam broth on a commercial scale), 1932, 1938, 1951, and 1963. The 1932 resurgence is still fondly remembered by some La Jolla old-timers who say that bean clams formed a staple article of diet during lean times, and they often refer to them as "depression clams."

To prepare clam broth, wash your clams thoroughly in running water for several hours, drain, then add one pint of water to each quart of clams and steam until the shells are wide open. Pour off the broth, add butter and lemon juice, and wish for more.

139. PURPLE CLAM — *Sanguinolaria nuttalli* Conrad. Length to 4 inches. Shells thin, rather flat, oval; right valve more flattened than left. Surface covered with a smooth varnish-like periostracum of red-brown color. Interior white with a purple tinge. Fairly common in sandy bays and estuaries.

140. CALIFORNIA JACK-KNIFE CLAM—*Tagelus californianus* (Conrad). Length to 4½ inches. Shells thin, flat, with umbo near the middle, and the long sides almost parallel to each other. Shell gray-white, covered with a dull brown periostracum. Lives in muddy parts of protected waters, where it burrows as much as 20 inches deep; when feeding, it moves to within 4 inches of the burrow entrance. Common. Widely used for fish bait.

141. ROSY RAZOR CLAM—*Solen rosaceus* Carpenter. Length to 3 inches. Shells thin, long, nearly cylindrical, with umbo near the end. Shell covered with glossy periostracum which is thin enough to allow the rosy

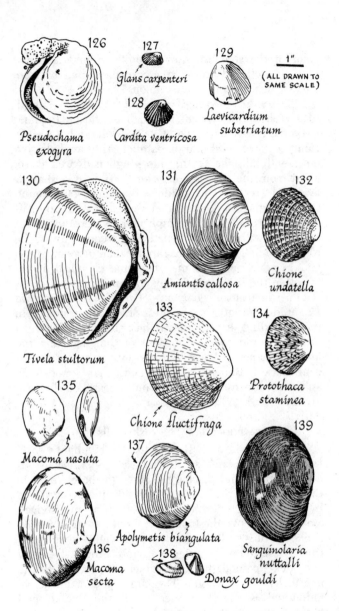

126 Pseudochama exogyra

127 Glans carpenteri

128 Cardita ventricosa

129 Laevicardium substriatum

1" (ALL DRAWN TO SAME SCALE)

130 Tivela stultorum

131 Amiantis callosa

132 Chione undatella

133 Chione fluctifraga

134 Prototheca staminea

135 Macoma nasuta

136 Macoma secta

137 Apolymetis biangulata

138 Donax gouldi

139 Sanguinolaria nuttalli

[109]

color of the shell to show through. Found in sandy mud in sheltered areas, in a permanent burrow from 4 to 12 inches deep. Not common.

142. ROUGH PIDDOCK—*Zirfaea pilsbryi* Lowe. Length to 5 inches. Shells thin, white, hard, fitting together imperfectly so that a wide gap is left at both ends. Long sides of shell almost parallel. Anterior half covered with file-like teeth; this roughened area is set apart from the smooth posterior portion by a shallow diagonal groove. This piddock lives in smooth round tunnels which it bores in clay, heavy mud, or soft rock. The boring is accomplished by movements of the shell, with the roughened part wearing away the rock; the shell grows more rapidly than it wears away, and in addition there may be some chemical action to soften the substrate. Fairly common.

143. SCALE-SIDED PIDDOCK — *Parapholas californica* (Conrad). Length to 6 inches. Shell rather similar to the preceding, except that it has no groove between the rough and smooth portions of the shell, and the long edges are not parallel; the entire shell is almost pear-shaped. Bores into hard clay, shale, sandstone, and other soft rocks along the outer coast. Fairly common.

Class SCAPHOPODA (The tusk shells)

These shells are all shaped like an elephant's tusk; both the large and small ends are open. Water is both taken in and discharged through the opening in the small end, while the larger opening is occupied by the large digging foot ("scaphopod" means "shovel-foot"). Just above the foot is the mouth, surrounded by a cluster of slender tentacles with slightly expanded tips. These tentacles wriggle around through the sand and pick up food particles, which are carried to the mouth by ciliary action. The larger end of an active individual is usually buried, with the smaller end pointed upward at an angle.

[110]

On both coasts of North America, tusk shells have been prized by the Indians, who often used them as a sort of currency. There are about 200 species, most of them in tropical waters; only a few are found in Southern California, and these are not common.

144. HEXAGONAL TUSK SHELL — *Dentalium neohexagonum* Sharp and Pilsbry. Length to 1½ inches. Color white. Shell slightly curved, with six prominent longitudinal ribs and a hexagonal cross section. Moderately common in offshore waters, but only dead shells are found in the intertidal zone.

145. POLISHED TUSK SHELL — *Dentalium semipolitum* Broderip and Sowerby. Length 1 inch. White, smooth, with fairly sharp curve. Very fine longitudinal ribs, running down from the apex to about two-thirds the length of the shell; cross section round. Dead shells not uncommon in coarse sand.

Class CEPHALOPODA (Octopuses, squids, and their relatives)

This class contains a number of groups which, lacking an external shell, appear not to be typical of the molluscs. Their soft parts, however, proclaim their molluscan affinities, and furthermore, one cephalopod, the nautilus, has a perfectly developed shell. Squids contain an internal "shell" — a stiffening structure known as the "gladius," and of a thin and transparent nature. The gladius of the cuttlefish is thicker and more chalky; it is the "cuttlebone" widely used as a source of calcium for cage birds.

Class characteristics include: a prominent head, with well-developed eyes; the foot transformed into a number of appendages surrounding the mouth, these appendages usually equipped with suction cups; the mouth with a radula and a chitinous, parrot-like beak. Development is direct, the young emerging from the egg with the appearance of miniature adults.

146. TWO-SPOTTED OCTOPUS — *Octopus bimaculatus*

Verril. Armspread to 3 feet, although this is unusually large. Color usually various combinations of gray, gray-brown, red-brown, yellow-brown, and black; color changes are swift and complete, and made according to the animal's reactional state. Fairly common in the low tide zone, in rocky areas.

The eight arms, or tentacles, are liberally studded on their inner surfaces with muscular suction cups. These are used entirely for grasping, and contrary to a widespread belief (propagated in the purplest of prose by Victor Hugo) neither they nor any other organs are used to "suck the blood" of their victims. Their prey is subdued by being held and bitten; the bite of many species (including this one) is poisonous, and such prey as crabs are quickly anesthetized by it. The two-spotted octopus envelops crabs in the umbrella-like web between the arms, and releases some of its poisonous saliva into the water that is also held there; this water passes over the crab's gills, and anesthesia is effected without the need to bite.

Some kinds of octopus bite rather readily, but this one is not prone to do so; my colleagues and I have handled thousands of individuals in the Aquarium-Museum at the Scripps Institution of Oceanography, and none of us has ever received a nip.

Another method of feeding has been demonstrated in the Aquarium. The octopus has a long, file-like radula, and with this it can bore through the shell of an abalone and inject its poison, causing the abalone to relax its hold on its rock.

The dangerous aspects of the octopus have been very much exaggerated, although there is no doubt that if a very large one should attack a man under water, there might be trouble. In general, a man is stronger than even the largest octopus, which the Marshall Islanders demonstrate by making a game of catching and killing 12-footers with their bare hands and teeth. The largest known specimen had a spread

[112]

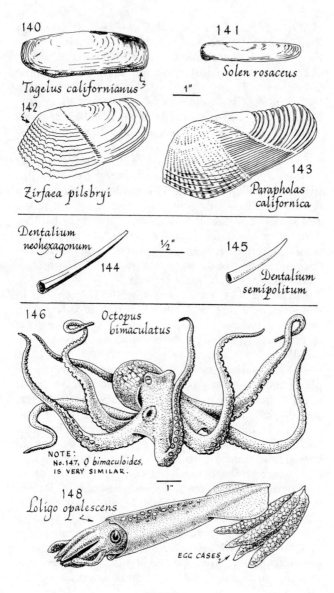

140

Tagelus californianus

141

Solen rosaceus

1"

142

Zirfaea pilsbryi

143

Parapholas
californica

Dentalium
neohexagonum

½"

144

145

Dentalium
semipolitum

146   Octopus
          bimaculatus

NOTE:
No. 147, O bimaculoides,
IS VERY SIMILAR.

1"

148
Loligo opalescens

EGG CASES

of 28 feet; taken off the coast of Alaska, this was a long, skinny species, and it did not weigh much more than the 12-foot specimens from the Marshalls.

Properly prepared, the two-spotted octopus is quite a delicacy, and this is partly responsible for its dwindling numbers. Its captors poison the water with copper sulfate, rock salt, or strong laundry bleaches, in order to drive the hiding octopuses into the open. This procedure is illegal.

Octopuses are well known for their possession of an ink sac which produces an obscuring cloud. In this species, expelled ink usually hangs in the water for a few moments as a discrete blob, and probably serves as a decoy to attract the attention of a predator rather than as a concealing smoke screen. It also has a chemical function in this species: it temporarily destroys the sense of smell in a moray eel, the octopus's chief enemy, which hunts by smell.

The octopus generally crawls on the bottom, but in moments of stress will hold its arms together in a streamlined shape and squirt water out of its respiratory funnel, propelling itself—tentacles trailing—very rapidly.

There has been much discussion as to the proper plural for the word "octopus," and the reader is invited to take his choice. One authority has said "The plural 'octopi' betrays an ignorance of three languages" in the thought that the word may be compounded of Latin and Greek roots. Some say it's all Greek, and that the plural should be "octopodes." Still others prefer "octopi," but maintain that the proper pronunciation is "oc-TOPE-ee." Because it has become a common word in English, an English plural would probably satisfy most people.

147. MUD-FLAT OCTOPUS — *Octopus bimaculoides* Pickford and McConnaughey. Common in muddy, protected waters. By all external signs, this species is identical to the two-spotted octopus, and may not be

distinguishable in the field. The differences are there, however; this one lays eggs that are several times larger than those of *O. bimaculatus,* and there are many internal anatomical differences. A significant fact is that each species has its own unique assemblage of mesozoan parasites.

148. OPALESCENT SQUID — *Loligo opalescens* Berry. Length to 10 inches. Squids are dwellers in the open sea, and do not occur in the tide pools. This one comes quite close to shore, however, and at night is often seen from the ends of lighted fishing piers. Dead specimens, and living egg cases, often wash ashore. But the best way for a visitor to see a squid is to visit a good fish market, such as those near the San Diego ferry landing, where they are sold, often under the name of "inkfish."

The squid has ten tentacles, two of which are extensible and occasionally much longer that the others. This animal almost never crawls on the bottom, but swims—partly by graceful undulations of the broad tail fin, but mostly through the use of its directable siphon. It can move forward, backward, or sideways with equal rapidity.

The skin of this squid contains various types of pigment cells, some of which (called "chromatophores") expand and contract, causing the most amazing play of colors over the skin. The color is never the same from one moment to the next; waves, bands, and spots appear and disappear, or wash along the length of the body. Another type of cell (the "iridophore") is constant, and produces the scattered areas of brilliant blue-green opalescence which give this squid its name.

The opalescent squid lays eggs in white, cigar-shaped cases about 7 inches long, often joined together at one end in small banana-like bunches; each separate case contains about 200 eggs. The whole thing appears to be made of stiff-jelled tapioca pudding. Great schools of squid come fairly close to shore to lay their eggs, and one can often locate these schools in the spring by seeing flocks of gulls (especially ring-billed gulls) congregated to feed upon the spent bodies of the egg-layers. The eggs are attached to rocks, seaweeds, or other objects, often in tremendous numbers. A fisherman friend of mine once had to recruit another boat to help him retrieve a shark net, which had been left in place for several days; the squids had attached so many eggs to it that one boat could not lift it. And Dr. John McGowan, diving in the underwater La Jolla Canyon in 1954, found squid eggs attached to the canyon walls in masses measuring 40 feet in diameter.

Squids are active predators, capturing and eating all manner of crustaceans, small fishes, and other creatures; stomach analyses by Gordon Fields and others show that they also eat each other, especially at times when many squids are found in a limited area. In their turn, squids are eaten by the larger fishes and by sea lions, and are used by fishermen as bait.

Phylum ARTHROPODA

The arthropods, or joint-limbed animals, are without doubt the most "successful" group on earth. In number of species, number of individuals, adaptation to a wide variety of environments, geographical distribution, and so on, no other phylum comes close to them. About 80 percent of all known kinds of animals are arthropods.

Their remarkable adaptive plasticity has led to confusing lines of relationships, and there is some disagreement as to the placement of the higher categories. Nevertheless, all show variations on a basic plan which is both simple and efficient. All arthropods possess jointed appendages ("arthropod" means "joint-foot") which show a wide range of specialization for specific functions, and which provide a basic key to classification. The entire body is covered with a continuous cuticle of a rather rigid substance known as "chitin." This is formed, in most cases, into plates or rings, with freedom of movement assured by connecting links of tough flexible chitinous membranes; the whole structure provides armor, and is an exoskeleton to which the internal muscles are attached. Growth in arthropods is accomplished by the periodic shedding of the entire chitinous covering, with all increase in size occurring in the brief interval between the removing of the old skin and the hardening of the new.

There are six or seven classes of arthropods, but only two will be considered here; the class Merostomata, (the horseshoe crabs) is not found in our area, while other classes, including Arachnida (true spiders), Myriopoda (centipedes and millipedes) and Insecta (the insects, and the largest class of all) are but sparsely, if at all, found in the marine environment.

Class PYCNOGONIDA (The sea spiders)

The sea spiders bear some resemblance to the land spiders, but the resemblance is only superficial; there is really nothing very much like a sea spider. It has a small body and eight long legs; internal sex organs branch into some of these hollow legs. There is no excretory system and no respiratory system. The circulatory system is a simple one, and assimilation is accomplished through a unique method of intracellular digestion in which certain cells lining the gut become engorged with food, then break loose and float about inside the body, allowing other mucosal cells to absorb their loads of food.

Some deep-sea pycnogonids attain a leg spread of nearly a foot, but the shore species are much smaller and quite inconspicuous. There are no vernacular names for most of these specific forms, and I have

[117]

not gone to great lengths to invent any.

149. SEA SPIDER — *Ammothella bi-unguiculata* (Dohrn). Leg spread to about ⅜ inch. Fairly common under stones in low tide zone; also found among several kinds of hydroids. This species was described in 1881, and has since been shown to have a cosmopolitan distribution: specimens have turned up in Hawaii, Japan, Australia, Europe, and North America.

150. SEA SPIDER—*Anoplodactylus erectus* Cole. Leg spread to ⅜ inch. Common among clusters of the hydroid *Tubularia,* especially in the Balboa region. The adult eats the hydroids, and its young burrow into the hydroids' digestive tract, there to spend their larval days as parasites.

151. ANEMONE SEA SPIDER — *Pycnogonum stearnsi* Ives. Length of body about ¼ inch. Total length, including the rather stout legs, about ½ inch, making this the largest local pycnogonid. Fairly common around the bases of the large solitary anemones, *Anthopleura,* as well among *Aglaophenia* and other hydroids. Color pale pink or white. Most common north of San Francisco, but fairly abundant in Southern California.

Class CRUSTACEA (The crustaceans)

The crustaceans constitute the most numerous of the marine arthropods, with about 30,000 species. These are divided up into a number of groups which we will call subclasses; some works, however, speak of the crustaceans as constituting a superclass, with a consequent elevation of our subclasses to classes.

The crustaceans are mainly aquatic in habit, and are characterized by the usual arthropod features. In addition, they have the crustacean feature of five pairs of appendages on the head. There is very often a median eye plus a pair of lateral eyes. The sexes are separate, and most of the young go through several complex larval stages which often provide the best insight to their relationships; that is, even when the adults are so different as not to present any basic similarities, the young forms are quite similar.

Crustaceans have a long and rich geological history, and a number of quite primitive forms have survived side by side with those more highly evolved. As we learn more about this group, its diversity becomes more apparent, and at least two distinct subclasses, not recognized before, have been discovered in the last 20 years or so.

Subclass BRANCHIOPODA (The fairy shrimps)

Most branchiopods are dwellers in fresh water, making their homes typically in ephemeral puddles and ponds. The adults die with the drying-up of the water, but not until they have deposited eggs capable of withstanding prolonged drought—years, if necessary—and the new generation begins with the next rain. The fossil record shows that branchiopods appeared in the upper Cambrian period, about 500 million years ago.

152. BRINE SHRIMP—*Artemia salina* Leach. Length to nearly ½ inch. The brine shrimp is able to live in water of extremely high salinity, and seems to thrive best in the brine pools of evaporating plants where table salt is extracted from sea water; the shallow pools at Chula Vista, for example, are literally swarming with brine shrimp. Because of their popularity as food for aquarium fishes, the general public is denied access to the ponds; collecting can be done only by licensed operators. Brine shrimp, both alive and frozen, are available at aquarium shops, as are the eggs, which hatch into naplius larvae as soon as they are placed in water.

One may occasionally find brine shrimp in natural splash pools high above the surf zone.

Subclass COPEPODA (The copepods)

In the open sea, the copepods are extremely important to the cycle of energy, as they form one of the primary links between the energy-capturing phytoplankton and the larger animals. Herring enthusiasts have spoken of the copepod *Calanus finmarchicus* as the world's most important invertebrate, since its numbers have a direct influence upon the numbers of herring.

"Copepod" means "oar-foot"; the feet of members of this group are adapted for swimming.

153. TIDE POOL COPEPOD — *Tigriopus californicus* (Baker). Length about 1/16 inch. Color red. Common in small pools in the upper splash zone. One must look closely to see these tiny creatures; watch for little red specks darting about.

Subclass CIRRIPEDIA (The barnacles)

For a long time, barnacles were classed with the molluscs, and it was not until 1830 that a British army surgeon, by observing their larval development, recognized their affinities with the crustaceans. A young barnacle emerges from the egg as a "nauplius" larva, then becomes a "cypris" larva; in the latter form, it swims about until it finds a suitable place to settle. It thereupon attaches itself to its chosen substrate by the back of the neck, secretes a shell, and becomes an adult.

Once settled down and grown up, the barnacle can do no more moving about. The population is spread, however, both by the free-swimming larvae and by the fact that many adults attach themselves to moving objects. Some kinds live on the bottoms of ships, for example, and some live only on whales; and one form lives only upon another kind of barnacle which is attached to a whale!

The name "cirripedia" means "feather-feet," and it is by means of its feathery feet that the barnacle feeds; the feet are extended from the shell, spread wide, and drawn through the water with a character-

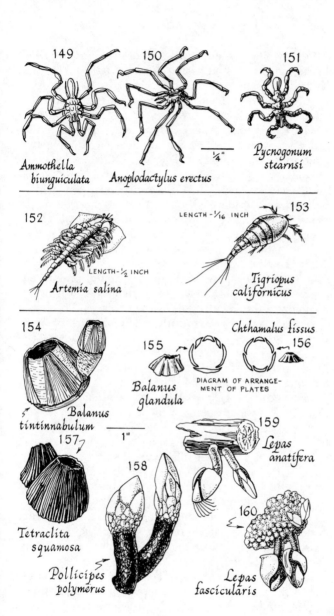

149 Ammothella biunguiculata

150 Anoplodactylus erectus

¼"

151 Pycnogonum stearnsi

152 Artemia salina LENGTH—½ INCH

153 LENGTH—¹⁄₁₆ INCH Tigriopus californicus

154 Balanus tintinnabulum

155 Balanus glandula

DIAGRAM OF ARRANGE-MENT OF PLATES

Chthamalus fissus

156

157 Tetraclita squamosa

1"

158 Pollicipes polymerus

159 Lepas anatifera

160 Lepas fascicularis

[121]

istic sweeping motion, then withdrawn into the shell to be divested of adhering food particles. This led Thomas Huxley to describe the barnacle as "a crustacean fixed by its head and kicking the food into its mouth with its legs" (*Anatomy of the Invertebrates*).

There are four orders of cirripeds, of which the order Thoracica is most important as containing the majority of the barnacles. The order Rhizocephala has only a few parasitic forms, while the Acrothoracica and Ascothoracica contain boring barnacles which will not be considered here.

154. PINK BARNACLE—*Balanus tintinnabulum* (Linnaeus). Diameter to 2 inches. The parietes (plates tapering toward the top of the shell) are red with white vertical markings; the spaces between them (the radii) are white, with fine horizontal sculptured lines. This is one of our largest barnacles, and is fairly common in the lower zones of rocky places. The feeding animal shows beautifully colored cirri of red, white, and blue.

155. WHITE BUCKSHOT BARNACLE—*Balanus glandula* Darwin. Diameter less than ½ inch. Color whitish. See the next species for further details (pls. 6*b*, 8*c*).

156. BROWN BUCKSHOT BARNACLE—*Chthamalus fissus* Darwin. Diameter about ¼ inch. Color usually olive-brown. This and the preceding species are not easy to distinguish in the field, as the color differences are not constant. The chief difference lies in the arrangement of the plates, as shown in the drawing. Both are found attached to any sort of solid object throughout the intertidal range and up to the highest splash zone, where they are wetted only a few times a year. They are abundant, often literally covering the rocks in some areas, usually forming a layer only one barnacle deep (pls. 6*b*, 8*c*).

157. THATCHED BARNACLE—*Tetraclita squamosa* Darwin. Diameter 1½ inches. Shape conical, sometimes slightly higher than wide. No obvious division be-

tween parietal and radial plates; surface uniformly roughened by deep vertical grooves and ridges. Color dark brick-red. Common on rocks and pilings in the low tide zone (pl. 6c).

158. GOOSE BARNACLE—*Pollicipes polymerus* Sowerby. (Formerly *Mitella polymerus.*) Total length to 4 inches. Like all goose barnacles, has a long fleshy "neck" which is attached at its lower end to the substrate. Extremely abundant on rocks and pilings, often growing in large clusters, and usually associated with the California mussel.

Goose barnacles have this name because of an old belief, held by at least one naturalist, Gerard (1545-1612), that geese hatched from them! In fact, the word "barnacle" probably referred to the goose (medieval Latin "bernaca") before it came to mean the crustacean. Present-day naturalists sometimes try to make sense of the common name by calling the crustaceans "goose-*neck* barnacles," but I prefer the name that calls to mind a charming tall tale (pl. 8b).

159. SHIP GOOSE BARNACLE — *Lepas anatifera* (Darwin). Length to 2 or 3 inches. This is perhaps the most abundant of the fouling barnacles, whose presence on the bottom of a ship can add tons of weight and create enough drag to cause the ship to lose half its speed. It does not live intertidally, but floating driftwood, boxes, bottles, and the like, may become literally covered with them and then be cast ashore. They are quite beautiful creatures, with clean white shells edged with bright red and blue.

160. FLOATING GOOSE BARNACLE—*Lepas fascicularis* Ellis and Solander. Quite similar to the ship goose barnacle, but smaller. The shell-plates are paper-thin. This is another high-seas species; it secretes a little raft of bubbles and floats about attached to it, without the necessity of finding a solid object to hang onto.

161. PARASITIC BARNACLE—*Heterosaccus californicus* Boschma. Seen only as a soft, shapeless mass under the

tail of certain crabs, especially the kelp crab (*Puget-tia*). The parasitic barnacle starts out as a nauplius larva, then becomes a cypris; in that stage, it attaches itself to a bristle on a crab's body, piercing it with its antennae. The barnacle's body has by then begun a process of degeneration, shrinking within its own skin, and it soon becomes small enough to flow through its own feelers into the inside of the crab. Migrating to a spot near the stomach, it anchors there, and grows a number of root-like extensions which reach throughout the crab. While the crab's outer cuticle is soft at its next—and what is to be its last—moult, one of these extensions pushes to the outside and forms the tumor-like sac under the tail. Great changes then take place in the crab; for one thing, it stops growing, and does not shed again while the infestation lasts. The sexual physiology is altered, and the crab does no more breeding; a male crab changes its shape, and develops most of the external attributes of the female, including a broader tail.

The barnacle itself absorbs its food from the crab's body, and of typical barnacle activities retains only the ability to produce eggs. These fill the external sac, and through a process of parthenogenesis—without fertilization by a male—nauplius larvae are set free.

The life of *Heterosaccus* is 3 or 4 years, and upon its death, the host crab may return to normal; most crabs, however, cannot live through the ordeal.

Subclass MALACOSTRACA

About two-thirds of the crustaceans belong to this subclass, which includes most familiar forms such as shrimps, lobsters, and crabs. The group is homogeneous in many respects, but extensive modification of every feature in the various groups makes the similarities sometimes hard to detect. The classification is necessarily complex. Many authorities recognize nine orders, distributed among five superorders, and must use such categories as "tribes" in order to provide effective groupings. We will consider only a few of the orders.

Order ISOPODA

With about 4,000 species, the isopods are an important group. The term "isopod," meaning "similar feet," refers to the lack of pronounced differences among the appendages; the legs are usually adapted for crawling or running and there are no large pinching claws. Some marine isopods are swimmers, some are burrowers, some are parasitic, and most are creepers.

The female carries her eggs on the legs or on the underside of the body, and the young go through the larval stages while still in the egg, emerging as miniature replicas of the adults.

162. SWIMMING ISOPOD—*Cirolana harfordi* (Lockington). Length to ¾ inch. Color gray, yellowish, or brown, with or without a pattern of darker blotches and spots. Abundant in tide pools, under rocks, among mussels, seaweeds, and so on, all through the intertidal zone. This little isopod is an important scavenger. It is equally at home crawling on the bottom or swimming through the water, looking like a fat little blimp.

163. SEA URCHIN ISOPOD—*Colidotea rostrata* (Benedict). Length 1 inch. Color red-purple. Found almost nowhere but among the spines of sea urchins, being most abundant in association with the long-spined *Strongylocentrotus franciscanus*. It is not a parasite, for it does no harm to its host, but simply takes advantage of an effective refuge.

164. KELP ISOPOD—*Idothea* (*Pentidotea*) *resecata* (Stimpson). Length 1½ inches. Color yellow-brown —just matching the seaweed on which it lives. On the beach, specimens are often found among masses of kelp that have washed ashore.

[125]

165. FLAT-TAILED ISOPOD—*Idothea (Idothea) urotoma* Stimpson. (formerly called *I. rectilinea*). Length ¾ inch. Color brown. This is a slow-moving form, and is fairly common under rocks in the middle and lower tide zones.

166. ROCK LOUSE—*Ligia occidentalis* (Dana). Length to 1½ inches. Color variable—usually somewhat matching the rocks on which it lives. The agile rock-louse runs about on the rocks in the upper splash zone, well above the highest tides. It is especially active at night, although some individuals may be seen at any hour.

Order AMPHIPODA (The beach hoppers and relatives)

Whereas the isopods are "depressed" (flattened from top to bottom), the amphipods are "compressed" (flattened from side to side). About 3,600 species have been described, and as detailed study of various micro-habitats proceeds, new ones are constantly being discovered. There are several suborders, the chief ones in our area being the Caprellidea (skeleton-shrimps) and the Gammaridea (beach hoppers).

167. KELP SKELETON SHRIMP—*Caprella equilibra* Say. Length 1 inch. Abundant on the fronds of kelp and other seaweeds, and also (with several other species) among hydroid colonies. The caprellids attach themselves to their substrate with their prehensile hind legs, and stand upright, making continuous forward and backward bowing motions.

168. MUSSEL HOPPER — *Elasmopus rapax* Costa. Length to ¼ inch. Abundant among clusters of the California mussel, where it serves an important scavenging role in the complex food chain of the mussel bed.

169. LARGE BEACH HOPPER—*Orchestoidea corniculata* Stout. Body length to 1 inch. Color brownish white; second antenna orange-red, not long enough to reach

middle of body when folded back. Two diffused gray spots on sides. Although often called "sand fleas," the beach hoppers have none of the bad habits of true fleas. They are extremely abundant on sandy beaches, usually staying above the reach of the highest waves at any given moment. During the day they either hide under seaweed cast up on the beach, or burrow in the sand. They are very active at night, and at times the upper beach in the beam of a flashlight will appear to be almost alive with them. Research has shown that they position themselves at a certain angle in relation to the moon's position.

There are several other kinds of beach hoppers in our area, but this is usually most obvious. *Orchestoidea californiana* (Brandt), with longer antennae, is quite a bit larger; it is found only north of Laguna Beach.

Order DECAPODA (The decapods)

Most decapods have ten feet, which may include a pair of large pinching claws. This is a diverse order, with some 8,500 species ranging through practically every imaginable aquatic or semiterrestrial habitat. Several groups are recognized, although there is some disagreement as to whether these groups should be called suborders, superfamilies, tribes, or series. We will consider decapods as divided into two suborders —Natantia, the swimmers, and Reptantia, the crawlers, and into tribes as shown below.

Suborder NATANTIA (The shrimps and prawns)

170. ABALONE SHRIMP—*Betaeus harfordi* (Kingsley). Length to 1 inch. Color usually glossy brown, although black and even blue ones are occasionally seen. Found living under the edge of the shells of abalones —usually one shrimp to one abalone. Occasionally seen among seaweed or in other habitats, but the abalone is the usual home. Very common.

171. SNAPPING SHRIMP—*Crangon dentipes* (Guérin). Length of body to 1⅜ inches; length of long claw to ¾ inch. Color dark brown and black. Common among rocks at extreme low tide. The thumb of the enormous claw has a suction-cup trigger which allows it to be snapped into a receiving groove with a surprisingly loud crack. Either the noise itself or the forceful jet of water from the groove may serve to frighten enemies; if this is actually the reason for the snap, these creatures must lead pretty harried lives, for a bed of them produces a continuous sound much like the crackling of a forest fire. You can hear this along any shallow water rocky reef just by putting your ears under water.

There are several species of snapping shrimp, and one or another of these is to be found in any suitable habitat in temperate waters everywhere. At least three kinds, of two different genera, are found here, but they are quite similar in appearance and habits.

172. STRIPED TIDE POOL SHRIMP — *Hippolysmata californica* Stimpson. Length to 1⅝ inches. Color translucent white or cream, with bold longitudinal red stripes. This is a graceful and delicate animal, abundant in the tide pools. It is especially active at night, and a number of them walking on tiptoe across the submerged rocks constitutes a characteristic picture of nightlife in a tide pool. They are easily located at such times by the ruby reflection of their eyes in a flashlight beam.

173. BROKEN-BACK SHRIMP — *Spirontocaris picta* (Stimpson). Length to 1¼ inches. Color usually greenish, transparent, with oblique red-brown bands. Abundant in tide pools and under rocks and among seaweed in the low tide zone. The spirontocarids, most of which have the characteristic bent-back appearance, constitute a large group of which at least a dozen species occur in Southern California; exact identification is not easy.

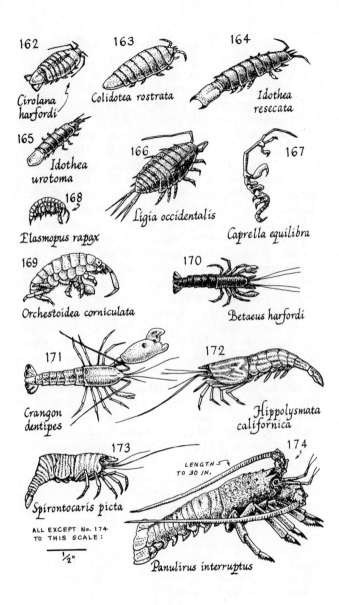

162 Cirolana harfordi

163 Colidotea rostrata

164 Idothea resecata

165 Idothea urotoma

166 Ligia occidentalis

167 Caprella equilibra

168 Elasmopus rapax

169 Orchestoidea corniculata

170 Betaeus harfordi

171 Crangon dentipes

172 Hippolysmata californica

173 Spirontocaris picta

174 Panulirus interruptus

LENGTH TO 30 IN.

ALL EXCEPT No. 174 TO THIS SCALE:

½"

Suborder REPTANTIA (The crawling decapods)

Tribe MACRURA

174. CALIFORNIA SPINY LOBSTER — *Panulirus interruptus* (Randall). Length rarely to 3 feet, weight to almost 30 pounds; tide pool specimens, however, rarely more than a few inches long. Unlike the Maine lobster, the spiny lobster has no large pinching claws, although the females have a small pincer on the last pair of walking legs; this is used to care for the eggs, which she carries attached to the swimmerets on the underside of the tail. It may also be used in fertilizing the eggs, by transferring sperm cells from the packet left affixed to her chest at the time of mating.

The lack of claws does not mean that this species is helpless, as anyone can testify who has grabbed a large one barehanded. The long antennae are thickly set with sandpapery spines, and when these are sawed across the wrist, the would-be captor is likely to turn loose in a hurry. There are sharp spines on the body, too, and the sawteeth on the under margins are especially dangerous; don't let the animal curl its tail on your fingers! Most skin divers wear gloves when catching spiny lobsters; it should be pointed out that the use of spears on lobsters is illegal, and the sports fisherman *must* use his hands.

There are other spiny lobster laws, concerning size and open season, and one should familiarize himself with these before attempting any lobster-catching.

The California lobster (or langosta, as it is often called) is an offshore form, but specimens temporarily caught in the tide pools are not uncommon.

Tribe ANOMURA

175. BLUE MUD SHRIMP — *Upogebia pugettensis* (Dana). Length to 4½ inches. Color blue-gray. A burrowing form fairly common in quiet, muddy waters,

but not often seen in the open. Its burrows are semi-permanent, and often a foot or more below the surface; their diameter is just enough to allow the mud shrimp to crawl through them, but there are always several widened "turnarounds."

176. CALIFORNIA GHOST SHRIMP—*Callianassa californienis* Dana. Length to 2½ inches, with large claw only a quarter of an inch less. This too is a burrowing species, and is found in a variety of substrates, going well up into the middle tide zone, where its burrows are often under rocks. The color is white, with blotches of orange-pink.

This seems to be a hospitable animal whose burrow is shared by a number of other species. Chief among these is the blind goby, a fish which appears in almost no other habitat.

The various legs of the ghost shrimp and mud shrimp are admirably adapted to digging, each leg doing a specific job, very like an efficient assembly line. Loads of mud and sand are clutched between the forelegs and carried to the mouth of the burrow to be dumped outside.

The ghost shrimp is widely used as fish bait. There are two or three other species, all quite similar.

HERMIT CRABS are familiar to anyone who has ever looked into a tide pool. All are well armored on the forward part of the body, but have large, soft abdomens. This construction would be a disadvantage in the hungry intertidal world, except that the hermit crabs always hide the abdomen in a discarded snail shell, leaving only their protected front quarters exposed. The abdomen even has a natural twist that corresponds to the spiral of most snail shells. The smallest individuals are often seen in little olive shells. As they grow, they move from one shell to another, always seeking a good fit, and the hermit crab's whole life consists largely of a ceaseless search for a more

[131]

stately mansion.

Almost any sort of hollow object will make a home for a hermit; some of them adopt straight worm shells, and I once knew one that lived in a pretty blue pill bottle! Whatever the shape of the house, the soft abdomen is protected while the armored wrists and claws provide a shield at the open entrance.

One species is selected here as typical of the group.

177. HAIRY HERMIT CRAB — *Pagurus hirsutiusculus* (Dana). Length to 4 inches in the north; in our area, such large ones are found only in deep water, while the tide pool specimens rarely exceed an inch. The antennae are gray or brown, and banded with white; there are no bands on the walking legs. Extremely common, especially in the shells of the black turban.

178. RED CRAB or SQUAT LOBSTER — *Pleuroncodes planipes* Stimpson. Length to 5 inches, color bright red. This is not an intertidal species, but once every few years great hordes of them are swept ashore to die. Their usual home is the open sea southwest of San Diego, where at times they cover acres of the sea surface. Quirks of winds and currents are probably responsible for their infrequent incursions ashore. Red crabs are a favorite food of tuna, and fishermen often refer to them as tuna crabs.

179. COMMON SAND CRAB—*Emerita analoga* (Stimpson). Length to 1¼ inches. Extremely abundant in certain localities. This is a plump little crab, about the size and shape of a jumbo olive; its color is pale bluish or yellowish white.

Colonies of these crabs inhabit surf-swept sandy beaches, moving up and down as necessary to remain in the area being washed by each wave. While under the water, each individual usually emerges from the sand and swims a short distance to a new spot, then, as the wave recedes, burrows quickly tail first into the sand, leaving only the "V"-shaped antennae showing. The point of the "V" points up the beach, away from the water. These antennae entrap food particles as the receding water flows over them, and there is just time to withdraw them and remove the food before the next wave arrives.

Sand crabs make excellent fish bait. Most fishermen claim better results if they use soft-shelled individuals, captured just after the shedding of the old skin and before the hardening of the new.

180. GIANT or SPINY SAND CRAB—*Blepharipoda occidentalis* Randall. Length to 3 inches. Color ivory. This is the largest of our sand-crabs. Unlike the preceding species, its first pair of legs end in sharp pinching claws; these are strongly flattened, and bear a fringe of "hairs." The front and sides of the carapace are armed with a number of sharp spines. This is a subtidal species for the most part, but south of San Pedro their shed shells are common among the flotsam on the beach.

181. PORCELAIN SAND CRAB—*Lepidopa myops* Stimpson. Length to 1 inch. Color iridescent blue-white. Rather similar to the giant sand-crab in shape, but in size is like the common sand-crab. It may be identified by the squarish shape of the front of the carapace, by its extremely long antennae, and its pincers. It is never very abundant, but is occasionally taken with common sand crabs.

182. THICK-CLAWED PORCELAIN CRAB — *Pachycheles rudis* Stimpson. Diameter of body ½ inch; large claw (which may be either left or right) almost the same size. Common in protected locations, as among mussels, in abandoned barnacle shells, in kelp holdfasts, etc. This is a slow-moving little animal, and, when exposed, may easily be captured; at such times, however, it is likely to resort to autotomy, and break off the large claw.

183. FLAT PORCELAIN CRAB — *Petrolisthes cinctipes* (Randall). Diameter of body to ½ inch. Color variable; usually brown, with bright red and blue marks

[133]

on the edges of the large flat claws. This crab has the appearance of having been cut out of paper, giving a flatness quite appropriate to its under-rock habitat. In the middle and low tide zones, the turning over of almost any rock will reveal scores of these little porcelain crabs scurrying for shelter.

Tribe BRACHYURA (The true crabs)

184. ELBOW CRAB—*Heterocrypta occidentalis* (Dana). Width of carapace at widest point is 1¼ inches. Found occasionally in sandy areas; cannot be mistaken for any other local species. It is a mainly tropical form, with Southern California representing the northernmost part of its range.

185. SHIELD-BACKED KELP CRAB — *Pugettia producta* (Randall). Length of body to 4 inches. Color glossy olive-green, spotted beneath with bright red. Found among seaweeds, especially *Egregia*. May be distinguished from the following species by its shield-shaped carapace and its smooth, glossy texture.

186. GLOBOSE KELP CRAB—*Taliepus nuttalli* (Randall). Body-length to 6 inches. Color purplish or brick red; surface of globular carapace usually of a dull "matte" texture. Claws may be very large. This is not an intertidal species, but is quite frequently washed ashore.

187. MASKING CRAB—*Loxorhynchus crispatus* Stimpson. Body length to 3½ inches, but usually smaller. The color is red, but the carapace is usually so covered with seaweeds, bryozoans, and other growth as completely to hide the red coloring. The crab deliberately plants these objects on its back, attaching them carefully to little hooked bristles. The environment is always matched; if moved to a new locality, the crab will divest itself of its old garden and plant a new one of local materials.

There are several species of masking crabs, most of them smaller than this one, and all very slow and deliberate in their movements.

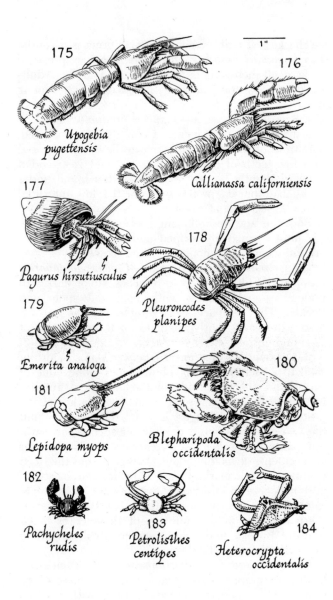

175   *Upogebia pugettensis*

176   *Callianassa californiensis*

177   *Pagurus hirsutiusculus*

178   *Pleuroncodes planipes*

179   *Emerita analoga*

180   *Blepharipoda occidentalis*

181   *Lepidopa myops*

182   *Pachycheles rudis*

183   *Petrolisthes centipes*

184   *Heterocrypta occidentalis*

1"

[135]

The largest crab of Southern California is a cousin, *Loxorhynchus grandis,* which attains a leg spread of at least 40 inches. It is not found intertidally. Adults do not follow the "masking" practice, but the young do.

188. RED ROCK CRAB — *Cancer productus* Randall. Width of body to 7 inches. Color usually brick red. The front of the carapace between the eyes is divided into five teeth of almost equal size, and is extended forward slightly beyond the eyes. Often found under rocks, half buried in the sand, in the low intertidal zone. Most active at night.

Both this and the following species have young that are most attractively striped and spotted, and these are quite common among rocks and seaweed.

189. SPOT-BELLIED ROCK CRAB — *Cancer antennarius* Stimpson. Width of body to 5 inches. Color dark red; undersides pale yellow with bold red spots and streaks. The carapace between the eyes is not extended forward. Fairly common, in the same sort of surroundings as *Cancer productus.*

190. MARKET CRAB—*Cancer magister* Dana. Width of shell to 7 inches. Row of blunt spines along edge of each hand (claw); inside of the hand and anterior legs often red. Color brown, somewhat darker at the posterior end. The longest legs are those just behind the two claws. This is a deep-water species in Southern California, and its occurrence ashore is a matter of accident; it is abundant, however, on the iced counters of fish markets, and is by far our most important commercial crab. Most of the commercial catch is taken in the north. There has been a recent sharp decrease in the numbers of these crabs taken south of Eureka, and some observers attribute this to the discharge of pesticides in San Francisco Bay.

191. SWIMMING CRAB—*Portunus xantusii* (Stimpson). Width of carapace to 2½ inches. Color blue-gray or brown. This crab is easy to identify, with its two

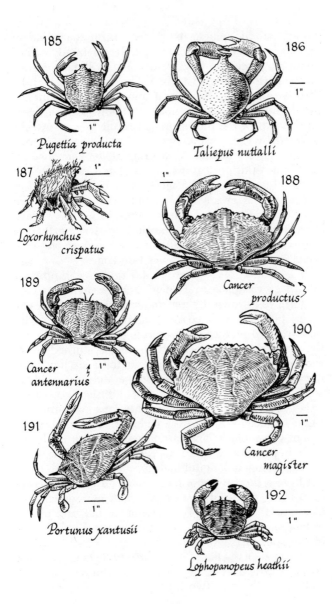

185 Pugettia producta

186 Taliepus nuttalli

187 Loxorhynchus crispatus

188 Cancer productus

189 Cancer antennarius

190 Cancer magister

191 Portunus xantusii

192 Lophopanopeus heathii

[137]

strong lateral spines, its ridged, razor-sharp claws, and its paddle-shaped hind feet. It commonly swims about in protected bay waters, but will take refuge on the bottom when disturbed. This crab must be handled with caution; the lateral spines make difficult the usual thumb-and-finger hold, and any awkwardness on the part of the picker-up can result in a severe cut inflicted by the sharp claws.

192. BLACK-FINGERED CRAB—*Lophopanopeus heathii* Rathbun. Width of carapace to 1 inch. Color extremely variable; perhaps the most usual color in the San Diego area is creamy white, but many red ones are also found. Fingers of the pinching claws are always dark, usually black, with the dark area *not* extended onto the hand. Common under rocks and among seaweed in the middle and lower tide zones.

193. LUMPY CRAB—*Paraxanthias taylori* (Stimpson). Width of carapace to 1 inch; usually smaller. Color uniform red-brown, lighter underneath. Carapace and claws pebbled with coarse granulations. One of the best ways to find a lumpy crab is to look carefully on the underside of a rock you have just turned over; the crab likes to hide in holes in the rock, and will not move out of them unless deliberately prodded. It is also found in washed-up kelp holdfasts.

194. BURROWING CRAB — *Speocarcinus californiensis* (Lockington). Width to 1½ inches. Color pale brown; tips of claws black. The carapace is squarish in shape, with a prominent spine at each front corner; it is convex along a longitudinal line, as if it had been cut from a short piece of large-diameter tubing. Abundant along mud flat waterways, such as those in the Corona del Mar area. Turnover of an old tire, plank, or boat on the mud flats will usually reveal individuals of this species.

195. PEA CRAB—*Fabia subquadrata* (Dana). Diameter to a little over ½ inch. Carapace almost as long as wide, smooth, with two blind-ended grooves running

longitudinally from behind the eyes to about half the length. This little crab is chosen here as a representative of the family Pinnotheridae, whose members habitually inhabit the gill-chambers of molluscs.

This one favors the California mussel and the horse mussel, and in some areas 80 percent of the mussels have a crab living in them. There is almost invariably only one crab to a mussel; males and females leave their respective hosts at breeding time, only to return immediately after breeding has been accomplished. The mussel-crab association was formerly cited as an example of a commensal relationship in which neither member was harmed, but recent studies have shown conclusively that the mussel *is* injured by the crab's constant picking away at the gills to remove food particles.

The males and females of the pea crab are very different from one another, as is the case with most crabs in this family. One pea crab common on this coast was formerly called *Pinnotheres concharum,* but this was shown in 1928 to be the male of *Fabia subquadrata. Fabia* had been named first, so her name became the official one—for both sexes.

196. STRIPED SHORE CRAB — *Pachygrapsus crassipes* Randall. Width of body to 2 inches. Color variable, usually showing transverse stripings; base coloring may be blackish, green, or red. The large claws are often red, and in any case are marked with deep red or purple veining. This is perhaps our most familiar intertidal crab, and is abundant on all sorts of beaches throughout Southern California. Although it does occur in muddy bays, where it hides along estuarine banks in holes made by the washing away of pickle-weed roots, it is more abundant among rocks. It seeks shelter during the day, but does not always get completely out of sight; a peek into practically any rocky crevice above the tide level of the moment will show a striped shore crab in hiding, with its red claws folded

protectively across its front end. If one is surprised in the open, or backed against a rock it can't get under, it will open its claws wide and raise them threateningly toward its pursuer.

These crabs are among the most effective of the intertidal scavengers, although stomach analyses have shown that carrion and trash do not constitute a very large proportion of their diet; their chief food is algae. Feeding is most often done at night, and the crabs look quite human as they literally shovel it in with both claws in alternation.

Like other crabs, the female of this species carries her eggs under her recurved tail. The eggs are yellow-orange, and ovigerous (egg-bearing) females are quite common.

197. PURPLE SHORE CRAB — *Hemigrapsus nudus* (Dana). Width of carapace to 1½ inches. Color variable, often purple or maroon, but never with transverse bands. Has fairly large red spots on the large claws. The two sides of the carapace in this species are almost parallel, while the striped shore crab has its sides converging slightly toward the rear. Both inhabit the same sorts of environments, but this one is likely to be more numerous away from rocks, and becomes more abundant to the north.

198. FIDDLER CRAB — *Uca crenulata* (Lockington). Width of carapace to ¾ inch; length of large claw twice that. The female has two small pinching claws of equal size; in the males, one claw is small while the other is grotesquely large. The large one is used in courtship and in fighting other males of the same species, and there is some evidence that its movements may constitute an elaborate set of communicative signals. If the large claw is lost in a fight or other accident, the small claw will become the larger one at the next moulting, at which time a small one will appear in the place of the lost big one.

Fiddler crabs make burrows in muddy-sandy areas

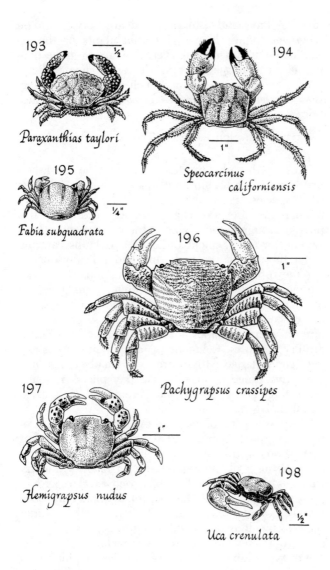

193 Paraxanthias taylori

194 Speocarcinus californiensis

195 Fabia subquadrata

196 Pachygrapsus crassipes

197 Hemigrapsus nudus

198 Uca crenulata

in quiet bays and estuaries, and are very abundant wherever found; like all the inhabitants of the estuarine environment, however, they are in grave danger of becoming extinct as the environment disappears. The burrows are as much as 4 feet deep, in sites chosen carefully to be above all but the highest tides.

Phylum ECHINODERMATA (The spiny-skinned animals)

This is the phylum that includes the starfishes, brittle stars, sea urchins, and sea cucumbers. All of its 6,000 species are marine.

There are several characteristics separating this phylum from all others. One of these is the ambulacral system, an arrangement of tubes and bulbs carrying water throughout the body and hydraulically operating the tube feet, which are variously used in locomotion and food-getting. All echinoderms have an internal "skeleton" composed of ossicles made of calcium carbonate; of microscopic size, these ossicles are often of strange shapes, and are often used for classificatory purposes. Echinoderms are unique in possessing "pedicellariae"; these are very small organs of a protective function, looking like tiny pliers or, sometimes three-jawed scoops, and are found on the external skin.

The basic plan of echinoderm anatomy is one of secondary pentamerous radial symmetry. This means that, although the larva starts life as bilaterally symmetrical, most of the adults attain a radial symmetry which is on a plan of five. The rich fossil record of this group shows that the plan of five has long been followed, and was a characteristic of the extinct classes as well as of the surviving four classes.

There are several classes of echinoderms. The class Asterozoa is divided into the subclass Ophiuroidea (the brittle stars) and the subclass Asteroidea (the starfishes). Other classes are Crinoidea (deep-water only), Echinoidea (sea urchins and sand dollars), and Holothuroidea (sea cucumbers).

Class ASTEROZOA

Subclass ASTEROIDEA (The starfishes or sea stars)

199. SHALLOW-WATER SAND STAR—*Astropecten brasiliensis armatus* Gray. Diameter to 9 inches. Color red-gray. The back is covered with granular rosetted spines of the sort called "paxillae"; there are enlarged plates on the margins of the arms, with prominent lateral spines. This starfish is confined to sandy areas, and is abundant on gently sloping beaches just beyond the breakers in water 10 to 20 feet deep; it is occasionally found in the lower part of the intertidal zone. Its tube feet are pointed rather than ending in the suction cups typical of the rock-clinging forms.

200. VARIABLE STARFISH — *Linckia columbiae* Gray. Longest arm not usually over 1 inch long. Color maroon, usually with gray mottling. All starfishes are good at regenerating lost parts, but this one is perhaps the champion. If it loses an arm, it sets about growing a new one immediately. Meanwhile, the lost arm itself may start to grow another starfish, and will be a complete animal in a few months. This new starfish is, of course, quite asymmetrical, with one very large arm and four buds; as if to even things up, the large arm will break off, leaving a stump more nearly equal to the other arms—and the cast-off portion will start the whole process again. This will continue until, after four or five "generations," the original arm is down to about ½ inch long; after that, it stays put. Even with all this effort, a pure radial symmetry is never obtained, and all specimens appear to be lopsided, and individuals with four, six, or seven arms are not rare.

201. WEBBED SEA STAR — *Patiria miniata* (Brandt). (Also sometimes called the batstar.) Diameter about 6 inches. Easily recognized by its flat shape, rough skin with scales, and bright colors. Colors range from almost white through yellow, orange, red, and purple-brown; some individuals are solid colored, while others have irregular mottlings and spots.

This species is long-lived in captivity. A group of about 20 individuals was known to have been placed in a tank at the Scripps Institution before 1936, and most of these were still going strong when removed to the new aquarium in 1952. At that time the identity of the group became confused with newly caught specimens, but I am convinced that a life-span of 30 years is not an unreasonable assumption.

The webbed sea star is found at middle and low tide levels in both rocky and muddy areas, is one of the dominant features of the kelp bed bottom fauna, and is seen by divers on the walls of submarine canyons at depths of at least 140 feet.

202. SOFT STARFISH — *Astrometis sertulifera* Xantus. Abundant in intertidal rocky areas. Often found under rocks. This species may be recognized by its limpness and flexibility, and its slightly slimy feeling brown skin covered with long orange and blue spines. The undersurface is bright orange. This is an active starfish, and uses its yellow tube feet to move with surprising agility toward the shadows. If roughly handled, it may autotomize, snapping off one or more of its long arms. It eats all manner of molluscs and barnacles.

203. KNOBBY STARFISH — *Pisaster giganteus* (Stimpson). Diameter to 18 inches. The knobby starfish is rather like the ochre starfish (no. 204) but differs in having larger and knobbier white spines, each surrounded by a bright blue aureole; the spines are scattered over the surface in no discernible pattern, and never trace the form of a pentagon on the central disc

as they do in the ochre starfish.

A close examination will reveal that the blue base around the white spines is in turn surrounded by a ring of brown fuzz; this is a concentration of pedicellariae, which will show their plier-like shape and action under low magnification. Their function is apparently one of protection from fouling organisms, although some starfishes have no pedicellariae and somehow remain unfouled.

This species is very common in rocky low intertidal areas, and ranges down to at least 100 feet deep.

204. OCHRE STARFISH — *Pisaster ochraceus* (Brandt). Diameter to 18 inches, although about half that is more usual. Color variable, ranging from pale yellow through orange and maroon to deep purple and chocolate brown. The spines, which are smaller than those of the knobby seastar, are arranged in a reticulated pattern of lines, and outline a pentagon on the central disc. Abundant in the rocky intertidal zone, but rarely found below the lowest tide level. Especially common in association with the California mussel.

Like many starfishes, this one feeds without actually swallowing its food. In eating a mussel it grasps the mollusc's opposite sides with the suction tips of its tube feet, and tries to pull the shells apart. At the same time, it turns its stomach inside out and holds it against the mussel's shell, near the ligamental joining. After a time, there is a slight relaxing on the part of the mussel, or a part of the hinge is digested away; at any rate, the stomach is further everted and slid down between the shells. An opening of less than 1/100 inch is required for the stomach to enter. The unprotected flesh of the mussel is digested and absorbed.

When this starfish is under water and undisturbed, most of the body between the spines will be seen to be covered with very small filaments, giving a fuzzy appearance. These filaments are extrusions of the lining of the body cavity, protruding through holes in the calcareous skeleton just under the skin, and are used for respiration. These skin gills have cilia on both surfaces, which move body fluids along one side and seawater along the other; oxygen is simply absorbed through the membrane into the body fluids. This method of respiration is common to most asteroids.

Another common asteroid feature that is well illustrated by this species is the possession of light-sensitive organs at the tips of the arms. These eyes cannot focus an image, but can distinguish between light and dark.

Many beach visitors wish to know how they may prepare and dry specimens of these starfishes. Unfortunately, there is no known means by which they may be dried and preserved with the color and texture intact. Boiling, with a subsequent slow drying in a warm oven, or exposure for several weeks to dry open air (not usually available in beach communities) produces a rather shriveled souvenir of a dull orange-straw color. Color photographs are far more satisfactory as memorabilia, and are much preferable from a conservationist viewpoint (pls. 7b, 8a).

Subclass OPHIUROIDEA (The brittle stars or serpent stars)

In the subclass (or class, depending upon whose authority you prefer), the central portion of the animal is a round disc, upon which the five slender arms are sharply set off. The arms themselves are very flexible, and in many species are fringed. There are little pockets in the disc between the arms, which serve as brood pouches for the young, and probably also serve as respiratory organs. The stomach cannot be extruded, and most ophiuroids feed on detritus.

There are a great many kinds of ophiuroids — indeed, they may constitute the most abundant group

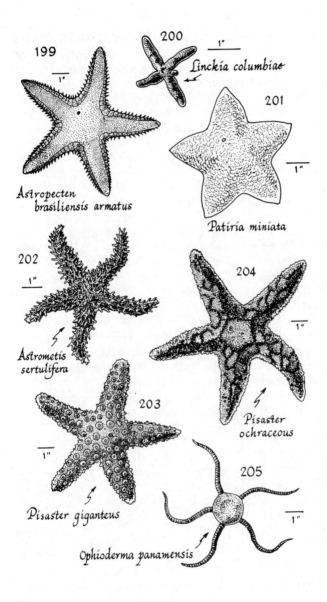

199

200

Linckia columbiae

201

Astropecten
brasiliensis armatus

Patiria miniata

202

Astrometis
sertulifera

204

Pisaster
ochraceous

203

Pisaster giganteus

205

Ophioderma panamensis

of echinoderms—but most of them live in the deep sea. Of those found in our area, identification is not easy, and their taxonomy needs revision; only a very few are here presented.

The term "brittle star" refers to the autotomous habits of many species, which will break their arms off at the slightest alarm; even the broken-off arms may continue the process, and break up into smaller and smaller pieces. New arms are grown from the central disc.

205. SNAKESKIN BRITTLE STAR — *Ophioderma pana-mensis* Lutken. Disc diameter to 1 inch, arm spread to 7 inches. Color dark brown, with faint light bands encircling the arms. Common under rocks, especially in a "rock-on-rock" situation, from the middle tide zone down. This is the largest local brittle star, and will submit to a certain amount of gentle handling without resorting to autonomy.

206. BANDED BRITTLE STAR — *Ophionereis annulata* LeConte. Disc diameter to ½ inch, arm spread to 4 inches. Color gray and brown, with salt-and-pepper markings on the disc, and distinct rings on the arms The disc bulges out between the arms. This species breaks itself apart rather readily.

207. SPINY BRITTLE STAR — *Ophiothryx spiculata* Le-Conte. Disc diameter to a little over ½ inch. Disc very thickly set with tiny, fuzzy spines; arm spines very thickly set. Arms unusually flexible, and autotomy is common. The color is very variable, and often beautiful, with orange-bordered bands around the arms. Individuals found in tide pools and under intertidal rocks often show the bright variegated colors, while those from deeper water offshore are almost invariably a solid deep red.

Class ECHINOIDEA (The sea urchins and sand dollars)

Members of this class are armless, and have compact globular or disc-shaped bodies of calcareous plates covered with spines; in the globose sea urchins, the spines are usually long and prominent, while in the flat sand dollars they are short and velvety. The calcareous plates form a shell that is usually called a "test," which is often elaborately perforated to provide openings for tube feet, breathing filaments, and the like. These tests, dried and bleached, are popular items at seaside souvenir counters.

The echinoids have a complex set of five jaws, which together form a structure known as "Aristotle's lantern" (although this term probably first referred to the entire test). These jaws come together at their pointed ends, and form an efficient tool for eating or, in some species, boring. So far as is known, Aristotle's lantern is not used for defense. Other defense mechanisms, however, are available, and some species, with poisonous, barbed spines, and venomous pedicellariae, are dangerous. Our local species are quite innocent in this respect, although the venomous *Centrechinus mexicanus* (Agassiz) has been taken in Mission Bay (San Diego) by divers.

208. PURPLE SEA URCHIN — *Strongylocentrotus purpurescens* (Stimpson). Diameter of test to 2 inches. Spines very numerous, rather short and blunt. Color usually bright blue-purple. This is our most abundant intertidal sea urchin, and is found all along the rocky coasts of California and northern Mexico. Apparently as a protection from the surf, this animal burrows into solid rock or concrete, and most individuals in open surf-swept areas have at least half the test well into the substrate. The burrowing is accomplished by motions of the test and spines while the animal clings with its tube feet to the rock; the motions may be an effort to prevent the urchin's being revolved by the whirling surges. Spines are quickly worn away, of course, by this abrasive contact, but they are being constantly renewed by growth, while the rock is not.

The holes become quite deep over a long period of time, and it is not unusual to see a sea urchin at the bottom of quite a respectable shaft; such animals hollow out a chamber at the bottom as they grow, and they are imprisoned for life. They are often seen on the outer sides of breakwaters, whether these be of natural stone or of concrete. And their presence on the steel casings of concrete pilings can result in holes right through the steel; the urchin keeps the surface clear of protective rust and growths, setting up a more favorable environment for erosion.

The food of the purple sea urchin is predominantly seaweed, which is masticated by the five-toothed jaws. Sea urchin population is very large at the bottom of the kelp beds, and they are very important in determining the comparative numbers of plants and animals. After the dying back of a kelp bed during the course of several unusually warm winters, the urchins' depredations were such as to prevent—or at least to delay—the reestablishment of the kelp bed. In an experimental tract, removal of more than a million urchins advanced the process, and the kelp came back. In the course of time, it is probable that the urchins would die back, of starvation, and the kelp get ahead again.

Young purple sea urchins are green; this has led to their being confused with the green *Strongylocentrotus drobachensis*, which is a northern California form.

209. RED SEA URCHIN—*Strongylocentrotus franciscanus* (A. Agassiz). Diameter of test to 8 inches. Spines long, pointed. Color red-purple. Common in tide pools at lower limits of the intertidal zone; more abundant (intertidally) to the north.

The gonads of certain sea urchins, which are eaten raw, constitute the "frutta di la mare" of Italian markets, and this species is popular among many Californians. The males are yellow and sour while the females are red and sweet, and a devout fisherman has praised the Deity for his thoughtfulness in providing these two flavors which can be used appropriately by poor people who would use sweet and sour wines if they could afford them.

Like most sea urchins, this one has two chief means of defense—the long spines and, scattered among their bases, the pedicellariae. If you touch an urchin with a sharp object, the spines will immediately bend toward it as if in an effort to keep it away from the test. If the touching object be larger and blunt, the spines will lean *away* from it, opening a clear path down to the test where the pedicellariae can take care of things.

The red sea urchin does not show the boring tendencies of the purple sea urchin, and is far less abundant in the intertidal zone.

210. SAND DOLLAR—*Dendraster excentricus* A. Agassiz and H. L. Clark. Test flat, 3 to 4 inches in diameter. In living specimens, the test is densely covered with tiny spines, giving a texture like coarse velvet. The beach visitor, however, is more likely to find the bleached test with its characteristic five-petalled flower design.

Living sand dollars occur intertidally only on protected sand flats; on open shores, they are beyond the surf, living at a depth of 20 to 50 feet—often in such numbers as almost to cover large areas of the sandy sea floor. When active, they stand on edge, with the lower ⅓ or ½ of the test anchored in the sand. Food particles are entrapped in sticky mucus among the spines, and this mucus is kept flowing by ciliary action until it passes into the mouth on the "lower" surface.

The jaw parts, Aristotle's lantern, are quite flattened; each of the five segments bears a resemblance to a white dove with its wings partly spread.

Many of these sand dollars support a single pink barnacle, *Balanus tintinnabulum*, on their upper surface.

Class HOLOTHUROIDEA (The sea cucumbers)

Most of the sea cucumbers are elongate, often sausage-shaped. They are soft and flexible, the skeleton being composed of separate microscopic calcareous plates; as in so many echinoderms, these plates are of distinctive shapes, and accurate identification often depends upon removing and examining them.

Tube feet are not present in all sea cucumbers, and when they are, they are never as numerous as in the asteroids and echinoids. Some tube feet have evolved into a ring of multibranched tentacles around the mouth, which are used in gathering food.

Respiration is by a method unique to this class; water is pumped into and out of the body cavity through the anus. On the inside, the water goes into a branchial tree which reaches throughout the body; the thin-walled extremities of this tree allow for the exchange of oxygen and carbon dioxide between the water and the internal body fluids.

There are about 600 kinds of sea cucumbers, some of them reaching a length of 5 or 6 feet. In the south Pacific, dried muscle-bands of sea cucumbers are made into "trepang" or "bêche-de-mer," a staple article of diet, medicine, and commerce. There are many species on the Pacific Coast, but only two are at all common in our area.

211. COMMON SEA CUCUMBER—*Stichopus parvimensis* H. L. Clark. Length to 12 inches. Color usually orange-umber; the surface is covered with warts surmounted by soft spines. The proportions and surface texture are very variable; harassed sea cucumbers are thick and firm, while relaxed ones are thin and flabby.

When handled roughly, or placed in stale water, these animals display a desperate sort of autotomy that is widely practiced among holothurians: they discharge most of their internal organs through the anus. The mass of discharged viscera is very sticky,

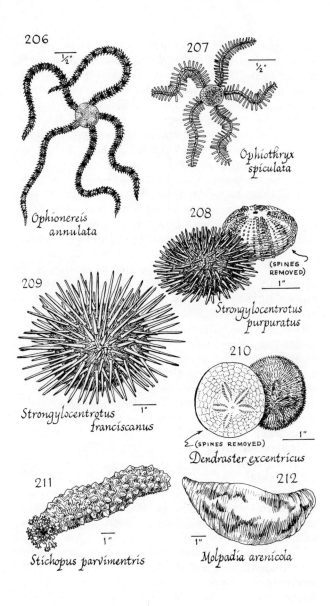

206

½"

*Ophionereis
annulata*

207

½"

*Ophiothryx
spiculata*

208

(SPINES
REMOVED)

1"

*Strongylocentrotus
purpuratus*

209

*Strongylocentrotus
franciscanus*

1"

210

(SPINES REMOVED)

1"

Dendraster excentricus

211

1"

Stichopus parvimentris

212

1"

Molpadia arenicola

and might well serve to entangle a predator, and the sea cucumber itself can grow a new set in 6 weeks or 2 months. The reason for all this is quite mysterious, as adult sea cucumbers have very few enemies, and this autotomy does not seem able to help the animal survive in stale water.

The common sea cucumber is seen intertidally at only the lowest tides. It is abundant among the rocks at the floor of the kelp beds.

212. SWEET POTATO SEA CUCUMBER—*Molpadia arenicola* (Stimpson). The term "sweet potato" is aptly descriptive of the size and shape of this echinoderm. It is smooth all over, with little wrinkles where it bends, and has no tube feet. The color is brown or reddish purple, with reddish blotches.

The sweet potato lives in sandy or muddy areas, apparently choosing a habitat just barely capable of supporting life, and only several special adaptations allow it to survive. For one thing, food is often very scarce, and the animal must be able to process enormous quantities of its substrate in order to extract enough food. For another, this area is likely to be deficient in oxygen, and the animal has evolved a blood system more efficient in using oxygen than that of other sea cucumbers. The respiratory pigment is concentrated in blood cells, as in the higher animals; *Molpadia* is one of the few invertebrate animals with this characteristic.

Phylum TUNICATA (The sea squirts and the salps)

In many books, this group will be listed as a subphylum of the phylum Chordata, and while there are some common characteristics (such as a stiffening axial rod called the "notochord," pharyngeal gill-slits, and a dorsal nerve tube), there are also good reasons for the separation, and the arrangement used here has been widely accepted.

One unique feature of the tunicates is their blood

flow, which operates on alternating current; it goes in one direction for a while, then the heart stops, takes a short rest, then starts up again propelling the blood in the opposite direction.

Class ASCIDIACEA (The sea squirts)

The sea squirts start life as rather advanced larvae, somewhat resembling microscopic tadpoles. When the time comes to settle down, they lose most of their advanced characteristics, and lose the features showing their relationship to the vertebrates. It is tempting to speak of this process as a degenerating one, but this is a loaded term; after all, the sea squirts are a very successful group, and are beautifully suited to their environment. From an ecological standpoint, they do *not* degenerate.

213. YELLOW-GREEN SEA SQUIRT — *Ciona intestinalis* (Linnaeus). Length to 5 inches. Color translucent yellow-green. This animal requires relatively clean and quiet waters and where these conditions are met, it is extremely abundant. The bottoms of floats and mooring buoys, and the sides of pilings, may be covered with a thick layer of them. Near the point of attachment to the substrate, this sea squirt is often covered with debris, but the two siphons are always kept clear.

214. LONG-STALKED SEA SQUIRT — *Styela montereyensis* (Dall). Length to 12 inches, color red-brown with maroon veinings; siphon-tips reddish-orange. Tunic tough, opaque. Lives in the low tide zone and lower, attached to rocks, pier pilings, or kelp. In quiet bays, especially in the southern part of our area, another species—*Styela barnharti* Ritter and Forsyth—is more common. It is stouter in shape, and has shorter siphons with maroon tips.

215. ENCRUSTING COMPOUND ASCIDIAN — *Botrylloides diegensis* Ritter and Forsyth. Forms a thin crust over rocks and other objects, preferring quiet bay waters.

Color ranges from red to maroon, with red tones the most common. Each individual member "zooid" of the colony is of pinhead size and pale yellow color; they are arranged in elliptical systems.

216. CLUB-SHAPED ASCIDIAN—*Euherdmania claviformis* (Ritter). Each zooid slightly over 1 inch long; club-shaped, united with its fellows only at the base. The colony as a whole may cover several square inches. Most often found at extreme low tide, the translucent greenish zooids hanging from overhanging ledges or vertical rock faces protected by other rocks from the full force of the waves.

Class THALIACEA (The salps)

These are free-swimming animals, inhabitants of the open sea, but are frequently found dead on the shore. They are almost completely transparent, and are usually barrel-shaped with an opening at either end. The inner organs are visible, although they too are so transparent as to require careful observation. The only opacity is in the visceral organs, which are often brightly colored, and form a small mass near the posterior opening. Salps breed by a complicated alternation of generation, with the sexual generation living in long chains or wheels of aggregated individuals, while the more familiar asexual generation is solitary.

There are many different kinds of salps in the Pacific, and their distribution has been correlated with certain water masses; their presence in a net haul may thus give information to the physical oceanographer as well as to the marine biologist.

The specimens found ashore at almost any time of year are almost invariably damaged and fragmented, quite often appearing only as pieces of tough, crystal-clear jelly.

217. COMMON SALP — *Thetys vagina* Tilesius. Length to about 7½ inches. Two prominent tail-like appendages on opposite sides of the posterior open-

[156]

ing. Like other salps, this one takes in water through the front opening, passes it through a food-getting filter, and ejects it from the posterior opening with a propulsive force.

Phylum CEPHALOCHORDATA (Amphioxus and its relatives)

Here again, this is often listed as a class of the phylum Chordata. The group has a few species of one basic sort of animal, often called the lancelet, which inhabits shallow waters and sandy shores in most temperate parts of the world.

218. CALIFORNIA LANCELET or AMPHIOXUS—*Branchiostoma californiense* Andrews. Length to 3 inches. Translucent, flesh-colored. Not often seen unless looked for systematically. Its usual home is in the very low intertidal sand on beaches surrounding bay inlets; it burrows to a depth of several inches. MacGinitie describes a collecting technique consisting of pushing a shovel blade straight down into the sand, then sharply jerking the handle back; this compresses the sand ahead of the lower part of the blade, and causes a nearby amphioxus to leap out of the sand. Unless it is grabbed very quicky, it will dig in again. Another method, all too easy to try, involves looking carefully inside discarded beer cans into which sand has drifted.

The name "Amphioxus," which means "pointed at both ends," was the official name for the genus many years ago, when it was thought that the cephalochords represented a direct ancestor of the vertebrates. We now know that they are an offshoot, a blind alley.

Phylum VERTEBRATA (Animals with backbones)

This is the phylum of most of the familiar creatures of the land and sea—the sharks and rays, the bony fishes, the amphibians, reptiles, birds, and mammals, each of which constitutes a class. Few vertebrates spend their entire lives in the intertidal zone, but many are to be seen by the temporarily intertidal human observer. There are no truly marine amphibians, and no marine reptiles are to be found intertidally in our area.

Class CHONDRICHTHYES (The cartilaginous fishes)

219. CALIFORNIA HORN SHARK — *Heterodontus francisci* (Girard). Also called bullhead shark. Length to 4 feet. The horn shark is quite common in the kelp beds, but is not often seen in the intertidal zones. Its peculiar spirally flanged eggs, however, are not infrequently washed ashore. Laid in pairs about 2 months after mating, these eggs hatch in about 8 or 9 months; the young do not go through a larval stage, but emerge as slenderer miniatures of their parents. Like the majority of sharks, this one is harmless, although its strong jaws could deliver a vise-like squeeze to a finger or toe foolishly placed in its mouth.

The peculiar shape of the egg has brought about a great deal of conjecture: "why?" Some say that if the egg is laid in midwater, it will spin as it sinks, causing it to become entwined in seaweed and so be kept from sinking into the bottom sediments. Others hold that the spiral flanges hold it up off the substrate, allowing free circulation of water around the main mass. We know that the shape, for whatever purpose, is successful, for hornsharks are numerous; on the other hand, other species produce eggs without all these spirals and flanges, and they do all right too. Perhaps the best explanation is that the female's egg-producing organs are constructed so as to produce this shape of egg most easily.

220. SHOVELNOSE GUITARFISH—*Rhinobatos productus* (Ayres). Length to 4 feet. Although frequently referred to by fishermen as the shovelnose shark, this is not a shark, but a ray. It is quite harmless, having no stinger and not being prone to bite, but it looks some-

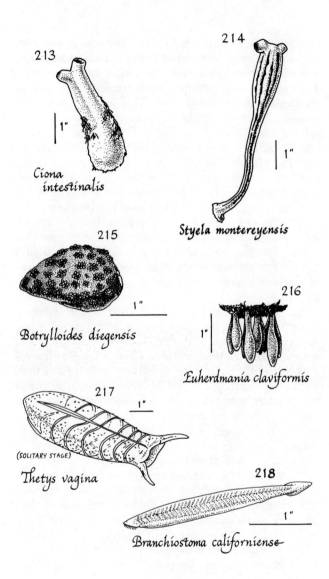

213
Ciona
intestinalis

214
Styela montereyensis

215
Botrylloides diegensis

216
Euherdmania claviformis

217
(SOLITARY STAGE)
Thetys vagina

218
Branchiostoma californiense

[159]

how fearsome; I have heard several visitors swear, after watching a large shovelnose being hauled in by a surf fisherman, that they would never enter the water again. The color is sandy brown, with transparent cartilage composing the pointed nose. This is an ovoviparous species, maintaining the eggs in the body until the fully formed young are born; the trauma of being caught on a hook sometimes starts the birth process, and 15 or 20 babies may be produced from a dying mother. At times, especially in the fall, the shovelnose guitarfish is extremely abundant, lying almost wing-to-wing on sandy bottoms just past the breakers.

221. THORNBACK GUITARFISH — *Platyrhinoidis triseriata* (Jordan and Gilbert). Rather similar to the preceding species, but smaller (not over 2 feet), with a rounded nose that is not translucent and three rows of prominent sawtooth spines down its back and onto the tail.

222. ROUND STINGRAY — *Urolophus halleri* Cooper. Length to 15 inches. Color brown, often marbled and speckled with black and darker brown and gold. Tail longer than the round body. This is the "stingaree" that brings the most grief to bathers in Southern California, and public lifeguards have to treat scores of stings every year. The sting is inflicted by a bone-like venomous barb located toward the outer end of the flexible tail. Stings, most of which are on the top or sides of the foot, are incurred when a bather steps on a stingray, which thereupon lashes with its tail.

If you should be so unfortunate as to be stung, try to find a big pan of hot water, and soak the injured foot in it; the pain, which can be extreme, will then go away as by magic. The wound will need cleaning, and you should arrange to visit a physician right away; while making the arrangements, and while *en route* to the doctor's office, keep the foot in the pan of hot water.

Prevention is preferable to the cure. Most of the

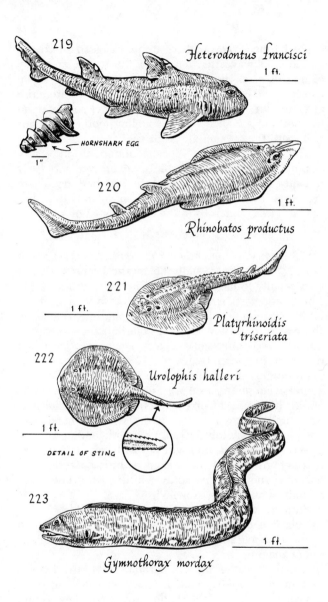

219

Heterodontus francisci

1 ft.

HORNSHARK EGG

1"

220

Rhinobatos productus

221

1 ft.

Platyrhinoidis triseriata

222

Urolophis halleri

1 ft.

DETAIL OF STING

223

1 ft.

Gymnothorax mordax

[161]

stings happen when bathers are jumping up and down in the cold waves as they enter the water, and they come down on the poor stingrays. It is better if you can grit your teeth and LET the cold water rise around your stomach, and keep your feet solidly upon the bottom; advance with a shuffling motion, and this will scare the rays up ahead of you.

The round stingray is most abundant on gently sloping sandy beaches in the late summer and early fall—just the time and place of the best bathing. There are three other species of stingrays in our area, but they are less numerous in the extreme shallows.

Class OSTEICHTHYES (The bony fishes)

223. MORAY—*Gymnothorax mordax* (Ayres). Length (rarely) to 5 feet. Usually below the lowest tide, but occasionally found among rocks in the intertidal zone. The younger specimens of a foot or so in length are most common in such situations, and these usually show a lot of yellow in their coloring; they are quite adept at wriggling snake-like to a new location when disturbed in their retreats.

Morays are not creatures to be trifled with, but their aggressiveness has been very much exaggerated. Most moray bites are incurred when a foolhardy lobster-diver investigates a rocky crevice with his hand, and finds not a spiny lobster but a home-defending moray. The bite is serious, and will probably require sutures; it is not true that it is a venomous bite, however, and it is not true that the moray will doggedly hold onto a victim until it has drowned.

Properly prepared, morays are quite edible.

This is a long-lived species: two of them (named Moray and Miranda) lived for 27 years in the Aquarium at Scripps.

224. KILLIFISH—*Fundulus parvipinnis* Girard. Length to 4 inches; usually smaller. Color olive-brown, paler below. Abundant in the shallow waters of sloughs and

estuaries. The killifish is a representative of a great and widespread genus, the various species of which are found in almost every part of the United States. Most of them live in fresh or brackish water, and many of them are very brightly colored. They make hardy and attractive residents of the home seawater aquarium.

225. GRUNION—*Leuresthes tenuis* (Ayres). Length to 8 inches. Green above, silvery below, with a broad longitudinal band of iridescent deep blue along the side. It closely resembles the related topsmelt (both are members of the silversides family, Atherinidae) but has the dorsal fin placed farther back, more than halfway toward the tail from the gill covers.

The life habits of the grunion are so unusual that many visitors reject a proposed grunion hunt on the grounds of suspicion of a "snipe-hunt" sort of practical joke. Grunion really do exist, however, and they really do "run" at predictable times, and may then be picked up with bare hands.

Grunion runs are always at night, usually on the second, third, and fourth nights after the full and new moon, beginning about ½ hour after the time of the highest tide each night, and continuing for 2 or 3 hours. The run may begin an hour or so later than this, and, of course, doesn't always begin at all in any particular spot; predictions show the time period during which they will run if they run, but there is no way of accurately predicting where the heaviest concentration will be. If grunion appear on the first night of a run at one locality, the chances are excellent that they will run in that same place, and more heavily, on the second and third nights.

The runs are the periods when the grunion lay their eggs: The female rides in on a wave, and while the sand is stirred up, wriggles backward down into it until only her head and the front third of her body are exposed, and she remains this way as the wave recedes. The male does not bury himself, but lies at the surface, curved around the female. As she deposits eggs in a little sand pocket created by her wriggling, he deposits sperm on the surface, from which it trickles down to the eggs. Both fish catch a subsequent wave back to the sea.

The whole process constitutes a marvelous adaptation to Pacific Coast tide conditions. If the eggs were laid before the high tide, they would be washed away in the rising waters. If they were laid a day or two prior to the peak spring tides, which come right after the full and new moons, they would be washed away a few days later. As it is, the eggs are not reached by water again until the next series of spring tides, about two weeks later, and by that time they are quite ready to hatch as soon as the water touches them, and the larvae swim out to sea. If the first spring tide after laying is not high enough, the eggs can wait without harm for 4, 6, or even 8 additional weeks.

Although limited areas of the beach may be covered with spawning grunion, the population is really not a tremendous one, and could be severely reduced by too many greedy hunters. Accordingly, the capture of grunion is controlled by law; the season is closed during April and May, and while it is quite all right to watch the grunion during that time, they may not be collected or interrupted. During open seasons, a valid California fishing license is required for all persons over 16, and only the hands may be used to catch grunion—no nets, traps, or holes in the sand. There is no bag limit, but conscientious collectors will only want to take as many as they may eat at the next sitting.

226. GARIBALDI — *Hypsypops rubicunda* (Girard). Length to 1 foot. Color, brilliant orange-scarlet. Baby garibaldis are sometimes seen in the tide pools, especially in the spring and early summer. They are about ½ inch long, at first, and are of a quite bright

red-orange with very brilliant blue spots. When grown to about 3 inches in length, the orange color darkens to maroon, but the blue spots remain; later, the bright orange comes back as the blue fades, and the adults have blue only on the very edges of the fins, if at all.

Adult garibaldis are not often found in the intertidal pools, but they may be seen from several high vantage points, as at Goldfish Point in La Jolla; looking down from the top of the cliff there, one may see numerous glints of orange as the garibaldis move. The color does not blend at all into the background; this fish lives near retreats in impregnable rocks, and has no need of concealing color. In fact, the color serves in the opposite capacity, as a warning and a challenge. The males have definite territories, and will savagely fight other males who encroach upon them.

The law forbids the capture or harming of garibaldis of any age. The young are sometimes caught for the home seawater aquarium, but this is illegal.

Giuseppe Garibaldi (1807-1882), the patron patriot of Italy, joined his fellows in wearing a scarlet shirt as a uniform. The fish may have been named directly for him, or at second hand for the popular loose-fitting garment worn by children and emancipated ladies in the 1890's, which was red and was called a "garibaldi" too.

227. OPALEYE — *Girella nigricans* (Ayres). Adult length to 15 inches; tide pool inhabitants, about 1 or 2 inches. Color light green-gray to dark blue-gray, lighter below; a single white spot (very rarely double) on each side, at the juncture of the dorsal fin and the back. The eye is, as one might expect, opalescent blue.

Adult opaleyes are abundant in their homes just offshore, among the kelp or along rocky reefs. Their eggs drift freely out to sea, and the young are born well away from shore. The young are slender and silvery, and as they grow they make their way gradually toward shore, at last seeking the haven of a tide pool;

[165]

once arrived there, they quickly metamorphose into small editions of the adult form. They remain tide pool residents until they have reached a length of several inches, when they seek the offshore waters.

These are active little fish, rarely still, and may be seen darting about in practically any tide pool. They are hardy in captivity, and make good aquarium fish, although their pugnacious habits are such that they should not go into a community tank with prize fishes of other kinds.

A common name for this species is "opaleye perch," which is all right as long as it is remembered that it is not related to the perches, but is our only local representative of the family Girellidae.

228. TIDEPOOL WOOLLY SCULPIN — *Clinocottus analis australis* Hubbs. Length to 7 inches. Color variable, ranging from pale greenish white to dark olive brown, always with spots and bandings of darker and lighter colors. Liberally covered with hair-like cirri.

This is a species that spends all its life in the tide pools, where it is extremely abundant. It is active and passive by turns, nearly always staying on the bottom of the pool, using its fins like legs for crawling and "perching," or swimming in short bursts to new localities.

This little fish is not related to the so-called sculpin, or scorpionfish, so often caught by pier fishermen, and is completely harmless. Like the opaleye, it adapts well to captivity, and makes a gentle and attractive member of a community tank.

229. SOUTHERN STAGHORN SCULPIN — *Leptocottus armatus australis* Hubbs. Length to 1 foot, although 5 inches is more usual. Color dark brown, sometimes with a tinge of olive above; lighter below; pectoral fins yellow, with several dusky crossbars. Skin smooth. Abundant in estuaries. The staghorn sculpin has a spine with a sharp cutting edge; this is located on the rear edge of the gill cover, and can be extended at

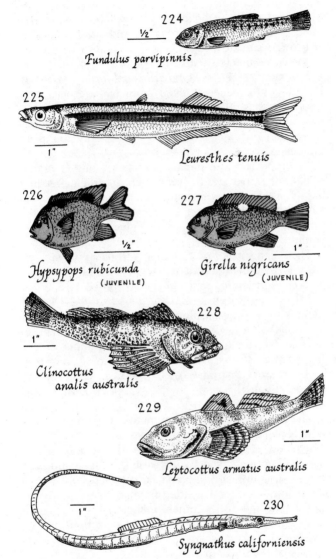

224

½"

Fundulus parvipinnis

225

1"

Leuresthes tenuis

226

½"

Hypsypops rubicunda
(JUVENILE)

227

1"

Girella nigricans
(JUVENILE)

228

1"

*Clinocottus
analis australis*

229

1"

Leptocottus armatus australis

1"

230

Syngnathus californiensis

[167]

right angles to the head; this makes the fish a very difficult mouthful for a predator, and presents a hazard to the human who picks it up. There is no venom, however, connected with this spine.

230. KELP PIPEFISH—*Syngnathus californiensis* Storer. Length to 18 inches or even more on rare occasions. There are several kinds of pipefishes in our area, but this one will serve to represent them all. All live offshore, and only dead ones are occasionally found on the beach.

The pipefishes are members of the family (Syngnathidae) that includes the seahorses, and their breeding habits are similar; the males have a brood pouch in which the fertilized eggs are deposited by the female, and later on the male appears to give birth to the tiny young.

There is a species of seahorse (*Hippocampus ingens* Girard) in this area, but it is extremely rare; there is only one authentic record in the last 50 years!

231. MUDSUCKER — *Gillichthys mirabilis* Cooper. Length to 8 inches. Color olive, marbled with brown or black. Skin very smooth and slick. Abundant in bays and estuaries but decreasing in number as the environment shrinks. It is a popular bait fish, and may be purchased alive at most bait stores; an increasing percentage of these specimens is imported from Mexico.

The mudsucker has a huge mouth, with parasol-like side flaps; the whole thing opens up to a diameter twice that of the body. Opening the mouth in this way has nothing to do with eating, but is connected with courtship, and is especially practiced by two males fighting over a waiting female. They open their mouths to the fullest, then ineffectually push each other with them until one appears to get tired and go away. It is a fascinating fight to watch, especially as neither of the participants is hurt.

232. ARROW GOBY—*Clevelandia ios* (Jordan and Gil-

bert). Length to 2 inches. Color light brown, with minute reddish and black spots, and a small blue-black blotch on the gill cover. This little fish is seen in puddles on mud flats, where it lives in great numbers; when frightened, it dives into holes and crevices in the mud, or simply hides in soft mud. Dr. Mac-Ginitie collected 425 specimens in a muddy pool only 3 by 7 feet in extent and 8 inches deep. As he points out, any animal living in such large populations must be an important ecological factor.

233. BLIND GOBY — *Typhlogobius californiensis* Steindachner. Length to 2½ inches. Color flesh pink, usually a little darker on the puffy cheeks. There are no eyes. This little fish was mentioned in connection with the burrowing shrimp *Callianassa* (no. 176), in whose company it is nearly always found. The pink color is the result of a network of blood vessels just below the skin surface, and these constitute an adaptation to the almost stagnant water of an underwater burrow; they absorb oxygen through the skin, complementing the work of the gills.

The gobies eat bits of seaweed and other detritus; they do not compete with the host for food, as the ghost shrimp eats only particles of very small size.

The blind gobies are nearly always found in pairs, one pair to one shrimp burrow. They seem to mate for life, although if one partner dies or is removed, the remaining one will accept a new partner. If an intruder of the same species happens into a burrow where a pair is living, it will be vigorously repulsed by both.

In spite of her small size, the female lays as many as 15,000 eggs at one time. The young have two perfectly formed eyes, but these cease to be functional within 6 months or so, at which time the goby finds a mate and settles down in a burrow.

234. CALIFORNIA CLINGFISH — *Gobiesox rhessodon* Smith. Length to 2½ inches. Color usually olive, al-

though it varies with the surroundings; three pale crossbands. Head broad and flat, with a prominent spine on the gill cover. All the clingfishes (of which we have several species) have an adhesive suction disc on the underside of the body, with which they cling to seaweeds or rocks. The forward part of this organ is formed by the pelvic fins, while the posterior is a fold of skin on the belly.

This clingfish is commonly found on the undersides of rocks, and doesn't seem to mind being upside down most of the time. The other local species are smaller, although it is possible that a 6-inch Northern California species, *Gobiesox maeandricus* (Girard), may occasionally wander this far south.

235. TIDEPOOL OCELLATED KLIPFISH — *Gibbonsia elegans* (Cooper). Length to 4 inches. Color matches the background, and is extremely variable; most often reddish, with eight or so vertical bands of a darker color. A diagnostic feature is the prominent eye-like spot, usually blue-black with an orange border, just back of the gill cover; there is usually a similar, but less prominent spot near the tail. This is a shy little fish, hiding in seaweed and eelgrass in the low tide zone, where it is abundant.

236. WEED KLIPFISH—*Gibbonsia metzi* Hubbs. Very similar in size and shape to the preceding species, but without the eye-spots; further, the color of this species is either solid brown or has longitudinal, rather than vertical lines. Most common in eelgrass, and the colors are most often silver and green.

237. ROCKPOOL BLENNY—*Hypsoblennius gilberti* (Jordan). Length to 5 inches. Color usually brown, liberally speckled with black and other colors. Superficially like the klipfishes, but this one is nearly round in cross section, while the klipfishes are strongly compressed. The rockpool blenny and its relative, the red-throated or bay blenny, *Hypsoblennius gentilis* (Girard), are common in the lower intertidal; they usual-

[170]

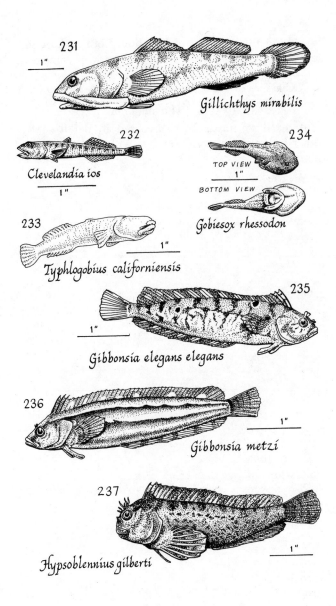

231 1"
Gillichthys mirabilis

232
Clevelandia ios
1"

233
Typhlogobius californiensis
1"

234
TOP VIEW
1"
BOTTOM VIEW
Gobiesox rhessodon

235
Gibbonsia elegans elegans
1"

236
1"
Gibbonsia metzi

237
1"
Hypsoblennius gilberti

[171]

ly hide in the seaweed at low tide. Both make excellent aquarium fishes.

Class AVES (The birds)

Class MAMMALIA (The mammals)

Both these classes are discussed in detail in two other books of this series, and so will not be discussed here.

SELECTED REFERENCES

Abbott, R. Tucker. *American Seashells*. New York: D. Van Nostrand, 1954.

Blackwelder, Richard E. *Classification of the Animal Kingdom*. Carbondale: Southern Illinois University Press, 1963.

Coe, W. R. Revision of the Nemertean Fauna of the Pacific Coasts of North, Central, and Northern South America. *Allan Hancock Pacific Expeditions*, first series, vol. 2, 1935-1940.

Cox, Keith W. *California Abalones, Family Haliotidae*. Sacramento: California Department of Fish and Game, Fish Bulletin no. 118, 1962.

Emery, K. W. *The Sea Off Southern California*. New York: John Wiley, 1961.

Fell, H. B. The Phylogeny of Sea-Stars. *Transactions of the Royal Society of London*, series B, vol. 246, 1963.

Fitch, John E. *Common Marine Bivalves of California*. Sacramento: California Department of Fish and Game, Fish Bulletin no. 90, 1953.

Hartman, Olga. Polychaetous Annelids from California. *Allan Hancock Pacific Expeditions*, vol. 25, 1961.

Hedgpeth, Joel W. A Key to the Pycnogonida of the Pacific Coast of North America. *Transactions of the San Diego Society of Natural History*, vol. 9, no. 26, 1941.

Hopkins, Thomas S., and George F. Crozier. Observations of the Asteroid Echinoderm Fauna Occurring in the Shallow Water of Southern California. *Bulletin of the Southern California Academy of Science*, vol. 65, no. 3, 1966.

Johnson, Myrtle E., and Harry James Snook. *Seashore Animals of the Pacific Coast*. New York: Macmillan, 1927. (A facsimile paperbound reprint was issued by Dover in 1967.)

Keep, Josiah (revised by Joshua L. Baily, Jr.) *West Coast Shells*. Stanford: Stanford University Press, 1935.

Keen, A. Myra. *Marine Molluscan Genera of Western North America*. Stanford: Stanford University Press, 1963.

Keen, A. Myra. *Sea Shells of Tropical West America*. Stanford: Stanford University Press, 1958.

Light, F. S., and R. I. Smith, Frank A. Pitelka, Donald P. Abbott, and Frances M. Weesner. *Intertidal Invertebrates of the Central California Coast*. Berkeley: University of California Press, 1954.

[173]

MacGinitie, G. E. and Nettie MacGinitie. *Natural History of Marine Animals*. New York: McGraw-Hill, 1968 (second edition).

Morris, Percy. *A Guide to the Shells of the Pacific Coast and Hawaii*. Cambridge: Houghton Mifflin, 1966 (second edition).

Osburn, Raymond C. Bryozoa of the Pacific Coast of America. *Allan Hancock Pacific Expeditions*, first series, vol. 14, 1950-1953.

Ricketts, Edward F., and Jack Calvin. (Revised by Joel W. Hedgpeth.) *Between Pacific Tides*. Stanford: Stanford University Press, 1968 (fourth edition).

Roedel, Phil M. *Common Ocean Fishes of the California Coast*. Sacramento: California Department of Fish and Game, Fish Bulletin no. 91, 1953.

Schmitt, Waldo L. *The Marine Decapod Crustacea of California*. Berkeley: University of California Publications in Zoology, vol. 23, 1921.

U. S. Department of Commerce; Coast and Geodetic Survey. *Tide Tables, West Coast of North and South America*. Washington, D. C.: Government Printing Office, published annually.

Walker, Boyd W. A Guide to the Grunion. *California Fish and Game*, vol. 38, no. 3, 1952 (Available from the Department in reprint form.)

Walker, Theodore J. *Whale Primer*. San Diego: Cabrillo Historical Association, 1962.

INDEX

[All references are to sections.]

[175]